LIFE UNDER FIRE

How to Build Inner Strength and Thrive Under Pressure

www.penguin.co.uk

Also by Jason Fox

Battle Scars

LIFE UNDER FIRE

How to Build Inner Strength and Thrive Under Pressure

Jason Fox

With Matt Allen

BANTAM PRESS

TRANSWORLD PUBLISHERS
Penguin Random House, One Embassy Gardens,
8 Viaduct Gardens, London SW11 7BW
www.penguin.co.uk

Transworld is part of the Penguin Random House group of companies
whose addresses can be found at global.penguinrandomhouse.com

First published in Great Britain in 2020 by Bantam Press
an imprint of Transworld Publishers

A CIP catalogue record for this book
is available from the British Library.

ISBNs 9781787633193 (hb)
9781787633209 (tpb)

Typeset in 11.5/17.25pt Adobe Caslon Pro Std by Jouve (UK), Milton Keynes.
Printed and bound in Great Britain by Clays Ltd, Elcograf S.p.A.

Penguin Random House is committed to a sustainable
future for our business, our readers and our planet. This book
is made from Forest Stewardship Council® certified paper.

To Jules: the final piece in the puzzle
as I rediscovered my inner strength

CONTENTS

Some of the battles and military operations mentioned in Life Under Fire *took place in unnamed war zones. The details and locations featured in those operations have been redacted to protect the security of those involved and the practices of the UK Special Forces.*

INTRODUCTION

LIFE UNDER FIRE

So how do we get out of this?

We were fleeing the scene of a bloody gunfight, running from the edge of a hostile village as enemy rounds ripped overhead. I looked around. Everybody was frazzled, a unit of men stranded in a remote outpost with nothing ahead but sand and rock for miles. Our landing zone was somewhere in the distance where hopefully a helicopter was waiting to extract us, but before that was five kilometres of potential ambush across the type of terrain Special Forces operators usually referred to as *deadly ground* – a stretch of exposed battlefield with very little cover and nothing in the way of escape routes. Walking across it was often a test of nerve. A daisy chain of improvised explosive devices (IEDs) might lie in wait; snipers in hidden positions could pick us off one by one at any moment; and there was every chance a mob of gunmen might give chase from behind us in Toyota pick-up trucks rattling with weaponry. But the biggest problem with crossing deadly ground was psychological: the understanding of an awful, inevitable reality.

We were all out of options.

We'd been patrolling and scrapping through the town in 45C heat for hours on end, as part of a heavy three-day operation. All of us were approaching breaking point and our squadron had also taken a handful of casualties. The wounded were inexperienced local soldiers working alongside the British military's elite forces and we'd been carrying them in pairs. One soldier had been shot in the arm, another in the leg. The most worrying injury was the poor dude whose gut had been torn through with a bullet. Blood pulsed from a hole in his stomach and he looked to be in a pretty bad way. I figured he'd live, but only if we could make it to our ride home in good time. The mood was jittery as we sprinted for safety.

I'd been in plenty of knife-edge situations like this one before – operations where the work had been tricky or helicopter crashes where I'd become convinced my time was up. During one operation, I'd been part of a team responsible for kicking in doors on a search for drugs and ammo. While I was moving from building to building, a gunman opened fire on me as I turned into a dead-end alley. Rounds ripped into the brickwork, drawing a deadly silhouette around my body, but I remained unscathed. Talk about a lucky escape. Now, moving across deadly ground, I needed some more of that good fortune, but the odds were stacked against me.

Weirdly, the mission that week had started out in a fairly routine manner. The aim had been to make our presence felt in a lawless outpost that intelligence had flagged as a hideout for fundamentalists and terrorist training cells. The town was located in an unfamiliar territory, one the British Armed Forces had yet to visit, and so we possessed very little information about what type of reception we could expect. Our arrival was completely unannounced and initially the mood among the local people seemed fairly agreeable. They'd been caught napping – literally: when we'd entered the town at dawn a truck of fighters had just slowly cruised towards us. The blokes inside, dressed in black robes with only their eyes showing through their headdresses, waved and seemed to smile, but I knew their AK-47s were in there too, stashed out of sight. Their leader made an obviously flimsy offer of cooperation. It was bollocks and we knew it. Once we'd kicked in a few doors and moved through one or two buildings – where we found stashes of guns, ammo and drugs – the mood turned nasty. An hour or so after we'd returned to our makeshift camp a few miles away, a loudhailer echoed instructions through the streets. Our interpreter relayed the highlights back to us.

'This will not happen again,' yelled the voice. 'We will engage the enemy when they come back . . .'

A fight was coming.

Our work on that mission followed a familiar routine. During the evening we usually grabbed an hour or two of kip under the stars at our base, having smashed into some known enemy positions that were located in the mountains nearby; during the day we made a series of routine patrols through the town to get a feel for the place. Our adrenaline peaked and swooped with the action. Given that we were at the tail end of a six-month tour of duty, where we'd been running missions pretty much every night, I was already at my physical limits. Sprinting around under the hot sun while carrying a backpack of heavy

3

equipment and weaponry had taken its toll. Emotionally I'd become a little frazzled, too. The stress of entering buildings unannounced and scanning the shadowy corners of dingy houses for gunmen and bomb-makers, while looking out for the safety of innocent civilians and screaming kids, had yanked at my nerves.

When the battle eventually came, it was ugly. We'd returned to the town the following morning for another series of door-to-door searches, but a different atmosphere had seeped into the disorientating alleyways and thoroughfares. As promised, there was a noticeably more hostile vibe and way too much activity for my liking. People watched us closely wherever we walked. A group of lads on motorbikes zipped through the streets, constantly checking on our progress, but this time their AK-47s were in view. It felt as if the first shot was only a heartbeat away until finally, at noon, I heard the unmistakable surge of bloody violence.

Bup-bup-bup. Bup-bup-bup.

Somebody was firing on the other side of the outpost. My earpiece crackled. There was a shout.

'Contact north of the village!'

More shouting came through on the squadron's comms network.

'We've got a casualty! We need to host a rendezvous point!'

I heard panting, the sound of soldiers running.

'Yeah, there's two motorbikes moving around with shooters,' shouted the voice. 'Foxy, we're coming to where you are. You'll see us in five minutes . . .'

Scanning the streets ahead for approaching gunmen, our unit

took cover. A few local soldiers, trained military personnel who were working alongside us, jumped behind the nearest wall. Others ran into a doorway. The buzz of roaring motorbikes and firing AK-47s was drawing closer, and my heart rate quickened as the oncoming gunfight played out over the comms. I'd found that one of the funniest things about war, or any horrendous situation I'd been faced with – those fast-moving life-or-death moments – was that the hearing, the imagining, of death or horrific injury on the radio was often far scarier than any act of violence I might have witnessed with my own eyes. An operator on the peripheries of a battle listening to the screaming and shouting through their earpiece could be more rattled than those lads firing in the thick of the action. I've heard it's the same for medics working in a frantic A & E situation. Doctors learning about a mass casualty event can be traumatized just by the anticipation of what they're about to see; emotionally they end up in a much worse place than responders helping any badly wounded victims at the scene itself. Without visual contact there's no context; the mind makes shit up, and any imagined story is far worse than the reality.

There was no doubt from the yelling in my earpiece that a nasty fight was kicking off, but I had very little idea how the engagement was taking shape, or its speed and scale. God knows how many people were shooting at us, or from where. I later learned that a group of enemy commanders had hidden themselves on a nearby hill. From above our position they were orchestrating the chaos with binoculars and walkie-talkies. One of them must have spotted my unit because a truck of gunmen suddenly turned a corner in front of us. The sky lit up, bullets chewed into the mud around me. There was a scream, then another. Two of my local troops had dropped to the floor. I returned fire, shooting into the side of the truck as it tried to reverse away, but it was hard to tell if anyone was killed in the exchange. Everything had happened so fast.

Bup-bup-bup. Bup-bup-bup-bup-bup-bup.

The gunfire drifted into another corner of town. As my adrenaline decreased, I heard heavy breathing – mine – and then the moaning of our two injured teammates nearby. One of them slowly rose to his feet and I noticed the bloody flesh wound to his arm. The other lad was in worse shape. At least one round had carved under his body armour, shredding his guts to ribbons. With the help of another soldier we dragged them both to cover, and a medic rushed over to patch them up as best he could. More British troops, retreating from the gun battle on the other side of town, soon joined us before climbing on to a nearby rooftop to pick off any advancing motorbikes or trucks.

Fuck. We're pinned down, I thought.

Our only hope at that point was if a Chinook helicopter could swoop in to CASEVAC (casualty evacuate) away the wounded – and us. But the response from our air support was worrying. Apparently we'd kicked over a hornets' nest. The local militia were fuming and any approaching choppers would make for easy target practice.

'We're not coming in there, it's too hot,' said one of the pilots. 'Get everybody to a safer place for us to drop on to, maybe the camp. We'll extract you from there . . .'

Bloody hell. I remembered our walk into town a day or so earlier and estimated we were around five kilometres away from safety. We'd need to run for most of that distance while carrying the injured between us. Meanwhile, an angry force might be at our backs, so we'd all need to draw upon every grain of emotional and physical resolve if we were to make it home in one piece.

Being up against it wasn't exactly a new experience for me. Emotional and physical suffering was something I'd learned to endure, and thrive within, throughout my military career. I had joined the Royal Marines at the age of sixteen and passed one of the British Forces' toughest training programmes, to become a Commando. Then, after ten years of dicking about during peacetime, in 2001 I signed up for Selection, the gruelling entry programme for the Special Boat Service (SBS), a wing of the UK Special Forces. The year-long assessment pitted me against the harshest of environments where everything seemed intent on ending my life: things with four, six and eight legs, the weather, even the bloody trees. Other obstacles were more familiar, more human; the aim being to test my motivation and mental resilience. The constant pressure and the standards demanded left me psychologically violated until I was deemed a suitable fit for what is one of the most expert combat units in the world. Several years of service followed where I operated at the military's sharpest point in some of the world's most dangerous war zones, fighting across a range of missions in counterterrorism, hostage rescue, counternarcotics and counterinsurgency. I was battle-primed for an escape like the one we were about to make.

Having worked as an SBS operator – the term we use for an elite soldier – for over a decade, I'd been driven forward by a sense of duty and a sheer bloody-mindedness to push on in extremely testing circumstances. The same stubborn streak would shove me on again as my unit prepared to escape that town, all of us considering our first footfalls in our struggle across the rocks and sand. I scanned the roads ahead for incoming enemy, expecting any second to hear the distant bark of gunfire again or the deafening *WHOOMPH!* of a landing mortar attack. Another epic test of endurance awaited me, for sure, but it was my job to survive and I'd been well trained in the art of resilience. I wasn't particularly looking forward to the run home, though. The work would be honking, but I knew I had it in me to complete the job successfully. There was no other choice.

Suddenly more orders came across the comms. 'All right, boys. We're going to have to move out quickly. *Let's go now . . .*'

The casualties groaned as we scooped them up by their arms and legs and navigated the narrow streets and alleyways away from danger; other lads dealt with minor injuries and flesh wounds of their own, but nobody grumbled. Instead, the unit moved purposefully as a circle, checking for incoming hostiles as we withdrew from the town. Every now and then we'd stop to engage an enemy fighter, the gunfire reverberating around the streets until, unexpectedly, two Harrier jump-jets swooped overhead, their approach called in by our Officer Commanding. It was an aggressive show of force rather than any attempt to neutralize the enemy. Given that there were civilians in the area, not to mention the fact that it was impossible to tell the good dudes from the bad on the ground, the pilots had to be absolutely certain before they could lay down an attack of heavy fire. I heard a *WHOOSH!* and saw a bright flash. Both jets had fired off flares, a warning sign to anyone thinking of continuing their pursuit as we left the town's perimeter. The fighters at our back soon slowed their pace.

By the time we'd begun our walk across deadly ground, my shoulders were in agony and my calves burned. Every muscle in my body was painfully taut. Somebody mentioned that the temperature had now reached 52C. I'm not sure if he was kidding, but it felt as if I'd been shoved into a pizza oven. There was no time for rest, though, and water breaks were out of the question, because we needed to move fast. If the enemy decided to open fire again, we'd be very exposed. I pushed on as quickly as possible, nervously watching the desert ahead for any unusual sand patterns or signs of disturbed earth, the subtle indicators of a recently buried IED. But that was only half the battle. My head was all over the shop. Even though I was relieved to be leaving in one piece, self-doubt burned at the edges of my thinking.

Fucking hell, I thought, looking at my wounded teammates. *Are all of us going to get out of here?*

But what was the alternative to putting one foot ahead of the other? Yeah, I could have moaned about fatigue, or slowed down the pace of our retreat so we could rest, but would that have achieved anything? I'd have become a liability to my teammates, and to myself, when I needed to be an asset. Any mistakes I might have made as my focus shifted to self-pity would have endangered the group even further. Instead, I leaned into my training and experience, breaking down our intimidating escape route into a series of easily manageable targets, such as a rock, or geographical landmark one hundred metres ahead. Making it to each one felt like an achievement, an emotional boost to keep me going. I'd mentally congratulate myself and then reset, scanning the horizon for another target.

Keeping only positive thoughts in mind, I pressed ahead through the dust and heat, each step drawing me closer to safety. I visualized sipping a cold pint of cider in a British pub; I even saw myself enjoying a day at the football. Concentrating on what was required to keep our unit safe became another distraction from the pain. I made sure to maintain my defensive position in the moving body of men at all times until, eventually, we made it back to the landing zone, where I knew the fight was done, both physically and mentally. I was spent, but we were away from danger. Squeezing into the back of a Chinook with dozens of soldiers, all of us piled on top of one another, bloodied, sweating and stinking, I finally allowed myself a settling sigh of relief.

Commuting, British military-style, had never felt so good.

How had I developed and grown to such an extent that I was able to operate effectively in some of the most hostile environments on earth? How had I become so resilient? Who or what gave me that emotional strength? And how much did it underpin everything I did? I understood that resilience was the voice in my head that pushed me on during a heavy gunfight. The same staying power had enabled me to live in the harshest of environments for months, as the environment rotted my body in the sapping heat and the wet. It took the same force of will to live in a cramped surveillance foxhole for several weeks on end with only a roll of cling film for a toilet, waiting for the slightest shred of counterintelligence that might prove key in a war against a dedicated enemy.

But where had that drive come from?

While I didn't think my inner strength was 100 per cent hereditary – even though physical power, speed and size can be passed on genetically – there was definitely an interesting lineage in my family that might at least explain why I'd moved towards the extremes of conflict. Both my dad's parents were involved in the military: my granddad was in the Royal Corps of Signals, while my gran was in the Women's RAF. On Mum's side, Granddad was in the Royal Navy, which he joined at the age of fifteen so he could serve in World War Two, where he was an engineer. (He must have fudged his application somehow, because he wasn't legally allowed to sign up until he was eighteen.) That sense of adventure was passed on and my dad eventually served with the Royal Marines. The stories he told me when I was a kid gave me an idea of what life would be like if I decided to sign up. Meanwhile, Mum was pro-military, having worked in the Women's Royal Naval Service. Nobody in the Fox family was surprised when both my brother and I decided to get involved in the scrappier end of life.

I imagine that emotional strength wasn't immediately obvious in either of us because nobody is born resilient. None of us instinctively knows from birth how to dig deep for mental endurance, or has the confidence to forge ahead through adversity when we're a little kid. I cried, hid and threw tantrums like every other toddler. But as I grew older, I learned that some of us become tougher than others because resilience is developed through experience. One bunch of kids might go on to live as fighters, able to cope in tough circumstances; others wilt as soon as life takes a nasty turn. But in both groups, their resilience – or lack of it – has come about as a direct response to past experiences and life-events, and what those episodes have taught them. So while DNA might give some people a head start when it comes to developing physical fortitude, there's nothing to stop anybody from creating a strong mindset.

Resilience certainly isn't just about physical power. Some of the fittest and strongest people I've known have downed tools whenever life has taken a rough turn. I also have friends who barely went to the gym but who became incredibly determined when presented with an emotional battle, able to push forward no matter what was happening. My grit, which was probably triggered as a kid somehow, developed through experience and specific training techniques in the military. In the Special Forces I learned to manage fear, emotional breakdown, pain in hostile environments and the horrors of war. I was forced to summon resolve during intense gun battles while negotiating the full spectrum of emotions – good and bad – because the alternative was to quit and die. For years, I felt comfortable in uncomfortable situations. I thrived in events that would have crushed most people, and work was a ten-year roller coaster of physical and mental extremes.

As an operator it was important to be resolute in three areas. Firstly, I had to be physically strong to cope with the challenges that a war zone might throw at me. I needed to move quickly while carrying heavy equipment and weaponry. Sometimes I was asked to climb on to fast-moving enemy ships, or to fast-rope out of a helicopter on to a target. Stamina was vital when moving in and out of high-stress operations, night after night, for days and weeks and months on end where I often worked having only grabbed a few hours' kip. Thanks to my training I was able to operate in the harshest of environments, and a lot of them were bloody horrible.

Mental resilience was also important. I often had to think on my feet in scary situations: spotting an escape route while bullets zipped about my head often made the difference between a successful resolution to a minor conflict or defeat; talking to angry and armed civilians rather than pointing a weapon in their direction was the best way to avoid a scrap. Despite what some people might believe, bloody gunfights aren't the default setting for an operator. (Though we are trained to excel in those situations.) Instead, I learned techniques such as 'the Grey Man', in which we blended into any situation by altering our actions and appearance. I know of some operators who even dressed up as homeless people on surveillance ops. Psychological resilience was vital to succeed in those roles.

The third and final component to being combat-primed was to show emotional intelligence. I wasn't a blunt instrument, immune to hurt and happiness, and a whole range of feelings could strike a person when they were operating in an area of conflict, a million miles away from home. I saw mates badly wounded – some of them survived, others didn't. The ones that were lucky enough to see another day discovered that their lives had been changed beyond repair and they never worked in the military again. In those grim moments I learned that grief had to be compartmentalized. It was no good wallowing in sadness or self-pity in the immediate aftermath of a friend dying in battle, not when a split second of distraction might mean that I was the next person being zipped into a body bag.

Sometimes a different type of grief dented an operator, especially when they were talking to people at home, when it was all too easy to become upended by an argument with a partner or to feel sad when missing the kids. I told myself that I'd only deal with the heavier feelings of life when I went on leave, because to do otherwise might have got me killed. The ability to turn emotions on and off was a skill that people in my position would often rely upon in tricky situations.

But I wasn't psychologically bulletproof.

My line of work meant that I experienced more emotional stress than most, especially during the intense gun battles that happened all too frequently. For years I was pitched into close combat where I saw people shot and blown to bits. I witnessed the impacts of war on civilian men, women and children, and later became ravaged by the fallout from our work. It was impossible to forget the mental scrapbook of war: the faces of innocent kids haunted me, their expressions frozen with shock after witnessing an outburst of hardcore violence. I became detached, depressed and stripped of any love for a job that had once defined who I was. My military mojo disappeared, my rage intensified. Weirdly, I was still able to physically function under pressure, even though my nerves had been shot through. For the first time in my career, though, I experienced real fear, but at no point did my psychological state endanger me or my teammates. The biggest problem was that my emotions were ragged.

Once I'd poured out my story to a military psychiatric nurse in 2011 – as detailed in my book *Battle Scars* – I was eventually diagnosed with post traumatic stress disorder (PTSD) and struck off from a job that had once given me kudos and identity. I hit my lowest point. My life was crushed by depression, by an overwhelming loss of self and by mind-numbing medication. Suicide seemed to be the only way out, but I pulled myself back from the brink. Later, my recovery from PTSD became an exercise in psychological endurance as I worked through a combination of counselling and personal rediscovery, learning painful lessons along the way. During my darkest moments I was encouraged by my therapist to think more like a kid by living only in the here and now: the past was done, the future was out of my control; I had to take one day at a time. Working in the moment helped me to refocus while the failures from my past became lessons, experiences to grow from. I was twisted all out of shape, for sure, but I didn't break – not fully. So if you want to talk about hitting rock bottom and surviving, I've got all the experience in the world.

And I came through because of resilience.

Thanks to my ingrained strength, I later found a new drive by working on TV shows such as *SAS: Who Dares Wins*, *Meet the Drug Lords: Inside the Real Narcos* and *The Final Mission: Foxy's War*. On those programmes I was placed in dangerous situations where I needed mental clarity to remain calm under pressure. Negotiating the full spectrum of emotions, good and bad, and managing my mental health became vital tools during moments of self-defence and productivity, as I built a new career for myself. Meanwhile, the psychological techniques I'd developed during my time as an operator still served me, both in and out of danger.

Throughout my recovery I learned that everybody has the potential to build fortitude – to differing degrees. Even if an individual believes they're short on grit or incapable of summoning actions of confidence and bravery in difficult situations, the truth is this: everybody can become resilient. Everybody can self-determine. Anyone can walk across their personal deadly ground and survive. All of us face internal conflict, both at home and work, even at play. Sometimes pressure threatens to crush us mentally. Emotional turbulence can overwhelm the mind until we feel unable to cope. Some of us might be struggling to overcome an intimidating personal challenge such as our first-ever 10K run or marathon. Others could be dealing with the death of a loved one, with addiction, divorce or debilitating illness. Then there are the millions of people coping with financial stress and unwanted behaviours. The consequence of failing to handle these internal wars can be catastrophic. Men's mental health is in crisis. The damning research from the Office for National Statistics tells us that in the UK around 17 blokes out of every 100,000 kill themselves in what has become a modern epidemic of mental ill health. While the women's rate is lower, at just over 5 deaths per 100,000, they are now twice as likely to suffer from anxiety disorders as males.

Life Under Fire: How to Build Inner Strength and Thrive Under Pressure lays down the techniques we all need in order to become more resilient in life and to discover the quality that's so important within the elite soldier: inner grit. It's very easy in books of this kind to talk about kicking down physical barriers and punching through glass ceilings. While those ideas will be dealt with across the forthcoming pages, I won't be telling you how to smash out one hundred pull-ups or the best way to nail a job interview. (Though you'll find inspirational techniques that might help.) Rather, this book is a pathfinder for locating mental and emotional strength while harnessing the desire and bravery to become stronger on a number of different levels.

From a career of intense stress and the experience of turning my shattered life around, I've learned how to overcome the toughest of internal conflicts. My challenges arguably began with the Selection process, where tests of soldiering and especially educational moments were set out in phases. *Life Under Fire* aims to tread a similar route: yes, the book can be read from cover to cover, but every chapter, or phase, within it can also be used as a standalone reference – a *break glass in case of emergency* option in sketchy situations when support or motivation is required. If used correctly, the lessons delivered here should help you to recognize and overcome your weaknesses by presenting new ways to structure your thinking. Elsewhere, the book breaks down key components in building mental endurance and inner strength. A series of instructional guidelines will help you to put into practice some of the theories I've learned, which, in times of stress, will provide the resources needed to calm the mind and operate successfully. Finally, I'll detail the warning signs to look out for when approaching rock bottom, before explaining the best ways to call in reinforcements and make your escape.

Life Under Fire isn't a bulletproof vest, a layer of impenetrable armour designed to shield you entirely from the shitshow in your day-to-day life. It won't help you to reach an unimaginable level of superhumanity either. Instead, the theories and techniques presented here reveal interesting ways of pushing ahead in situations when the thought of taking another step might seem impossible. It explains new methods for rising up again after failure while emerging a stronger person. It locates the thought processes and practices required in order to become fortified, braver and so much harder to break.

My experiences have taught me that life can be a war zone, so we should all prepare accordingly.

This book will show you how.

PART ONE

THE BATTLE MIND

HOW TO FIND RESILIENCE

AUTHOR'S NOTE

Life Under Fire is split into two parts. The first, 'The Battle Mind', delivers the background required to develop resilient thought. When the action kicks off for real, Part Two, 'By Strength and Guile', is there to impart some of the procedures and practices required for ensuring success. Every chapter within them is an individual phase of learning designed to instil resilience and inform tactical thinking. In many ways, each chapter mirrors the experience of development endured by a lot of elite operators from when they first enter the regular military: this begins with a period of Basic Training and is followed by the introduction of increasingly advanced manoeuvres and strategies throughout an individual's career until the more expert and experienced soldiers undergo Selection and join the Special Forces.

During my time in the military it became apparent that five key factors needed to be in place if I were to be resolute about surviving: purpose, experience, the existence of a brotherhood, self-awareness, and honesty and acceptance of a bad situation were vital tools in my armoury. I applied them as follows.

1) Purpose: While at war, my cause was fighting the good fight. I told myself that I was keeping bad people from training other bad people who wanted to commit atrocities in places where my friends and family might be at risk.

2) Experience: This was the mental fuel that told me I could handle any situation, even if I'd never previously been in that position.

3) Brotherhood: I was helped through some sketchy moments with the knowledge that everybody around me was highly skilled, motivated and willing to take a bullet for me if an operation took an ugly turn.

4) Self-awareness: I had a clear understanding of where my breaking point was and had learned how I could move past it, which allowed me to function effectively, for longer.

5) Honesty and acceptance of a bad situation: I acknowledged when I was in a bad place and tried to react positively, without pessimism or negative thought. It became the quickest way to get the job done. Meanwhile, denial was a destructive enemy.

These five factors became my building blocks of resilience, the fundamental steps I took to ensure a robust state of mind as I moved into elite military service. I'll detail them all in Part One of the book and with the right level of Basic Training they will provide the foundations for fortitude. All the processes can be applied to any situation or challenge, and by implementing a little planning or psychological rewiring you'll find that each step can be integrated fairly easily into your life.

It's important to know that each building block is equally valuable and that the list doesn't necessarily have to be implemented in the order set out here. But by working through all the stages you'll soon develop the skills to negotiate any event that requires a resilient mindset.

PHASE ONE

BASIC TRAINING:
THE COMMANDO SPIRIT

Resilience: what is it?

According to the Oxford English Dictionary, it's the ability to return quickly from illness, change or misfortune. Premier League managers might describe it as 'bouncebackability' – the desire to get back up after a heavy defeat or bad luck. But in the military we think of it as Not Quitting, of pushing on to the end, which is a vital asset in combat. Military operators with high levels of resilience survive in gun battles. They lead in desperate situations. They're able to think on their feet with only a few moments to plan and then execute those plans effectively. They deal with periods of physical and emotional discomfort and they function expertly even when the end isn't in sight.

Resilience is the heartbeat of everything we do in the military, especially at the specialist level where there's very little room for error or mental weakness. Resilience is what keeps an individual going when bad shit happens. Without it, there's every chance a soldier might flap or spin out at the worst possible moment, such as in the heat of a gunfight, when sharp minds and bravery are required. In a situation of that nature, a less resilient person becomes a liability. They might die as a result, or quit when their teammates need them to stay strong. Even worse, as the weakest link in the chain, it's possible they might also cause others to be killed and the implications of their failures are huge. If troops on the ground can't execute the tasks at hand, the smaller conflicts and bigger battles are given away until, eventually, the war is lost.

The only way to reduce the odds of failure is to instil as much resilience as possible in every man and woman working through their military training. That process begins on the very first minute of the very first day of service.

It takes a fair bit of physical and psychological pain to become resilient. The long-distance swimmer hoping to cross the English Channel will have to face some mega-honking training sessions if they're to succeed. A first-time parent might endure countless sleepless nights, moments of crippling self-doubt and bouts of depression. Elsewhere, the owner of a start-up business can receive rejections, criticism and any number of financial hits. But whenever the pain arrives – the aching muscles, the screaming baby, the horrific tax bill – there are always two basic choices.

1) Quit.
2) Get up and crack on.

I've learned through my experiences, in and out of the military, that every blow leaves a wound. But every wound forms a scar. Every scar acts as a reminder that the pain, no matter how awful, is temporary and that progress has always followed whenever I've pressed ahead, regardless of how scared or hurt I was. That's the nuts and bolts of resilience. Only by enduring those painful training sessions can the wannabe long-distance swimmer reach the physical levels required to swim the English Channel. By coping with the tears and tantrums, the first-time parent learns how to better survive those difficult early months should they later go for kids two and three, as well as the years that follow. And through financial struggle, the start-up entrepreneur understands how to see their vision through to the end.

In the military I took a lot of psychological and physical hits. I have a lot of scars. And each one left me stronger than before.

My personal thrashing began as a sixteen-year-old, when I signed up to become a Commando on the Potential Recruits Course – now known as the Potential Royal Marines Course (PRMC) – in 1992. When it comes to taking the first steps to building resilience, there's no better place to look than the Royal Marines, which boasts one of the toughest military training courses in the world. Much of that reputation is down to the Commando Spirit: a code of conduct drummed into every potential recruit when they arrive for their first day of Basic Training, a thirty-two-week programme comprising an education in all the skills required in combat.

For any potential Marine hoping to build resilience, the Commando Spirit is a vital educational tool and has four cornerstones that must be learned if they're to make it to the end of training:

1) Courage: get out front and do what's right.
2) Determination: never give up.
3) Unselfishness: opposite number (oppo) first, team second, self last.

And finally,

4) Cheerfulness in the face of adversity: make humour the heart of morale.

During training, these four ideals help to instil physical and emotional robustness in everyone open to learning them. In conflict, they provide the Marines with an armoury of psychological and physical weapons, each cornerstone emboldening them to overcome the toughest challenges war can chuck their way. I know because they helped me to survive some pretty hairy situations. Without the Commando Spirit, it's unlikely I would have progressed into the sharp end of military life and survived the hardships that threatened to overcome me during combat situations. Had those values not been instilled in me, it's also more than likely I would have been crushed by the emotional fallout to my elite career once I'd been medically discharged with PTSD.

From the off, every recruit is bombarded with the Commando Spirit. Posters and signs are pinned everywhere at the Commando Training Centre Royal Marines near Lympstone in Devon. Slogans are painted on gym walls. Reminders are written in books, mentioned in talks and shouted out during the series of lengthy runs across muddy ground in the pissing wet as everybody struggles with the weight of full combat kit. At no point is a recruit allowed to forget the importance of the

Commando Spirit. Those ideals are essential to building resilience, and very quickly they become the foundation for everything that follows, both in real-life combat and peacekeeping. Anyone who isn't able to take them on is rooted out during training and given the boot, because understanding how to implement the Commando Spirit is as important as learning how to fire a weapon or maintaining the required levels of personal admin, such as appearance and preparedness. Starting towards a resilient mind requires everybody to familiarize themselves with all four elements – no exceptions, no excuses.

Just as importantly, I was also taught that the basic application of courage, determination, unselfishness and cheerfulness in the face of adversity could prove equally effective beyond my experiences in the Royal Marines, and the Commando Spirit was a key that would help me to unlock the resilience required to succeed in any challenge, no matter its size or scale. Everybody has the capacity to develop these attitudes, but the first step is to understand how the military instil them at the start.

#1 COURAGE
GET OUT FRONT AND DO WHAT'S RIGHT

How the hell do you teach courage? It's an age-old question that the Royal Marines have answered with a simple methodology: they take every individual hoping to make it as a Commando and shove them out of their comfort zone. When I was starting out as a sixteen-year-old recruit, some of the lads around me wilted under pressure, but a hell of a lot more survived. Those that did, including me, toughened up as a result, and as a style of teaching it was one that everybody could learn from because the results it generated were so powerful.

Prior to signing up for Basic Training, my military experience was fairly limited. Dad, having been a Marine himself, was big on teaching my brother and me the basics of map-reading, so I had a vague idea of how to handle myself outdoors. I was a strong lad and I loved sport, so physically I was pretty fit too. As for the rest of it? I didn't have a bloody clue. When I was dropped off for the first day of my new life, I was a naive and scrawny teenage dweeb and I was immediately exposed to some very harsh lessons about life in the Marines, as were the rest of the troop I'd joined up with.

Having barely settled into our new surroundings, we were thrown into the deep end on a daily basis, where the bare minimum expected of us was to not drown. I guess the trainers at Lympstone believed we must be fairly tough individuals, given that we'd signed up to become Marines in the first place. They understood that everyone had a certain level of courage in them and they were determined to discover just how much we carried. I was challenged physically and psychologically during a series of tests that increased in intensity and technical skill. Often, at the news of our latest daunting adventure – such as a long run while carrying full combat load – the natural reaction was to think, *I can't bloody do that!* The training staff's response to any flashes of self-doubt was to say firmly, 'Yes, you bloody can do it. And you will – at seven o'clock tomorrow morning.' It forced everybody to rise to the challenge. The ones that couldn't hack it usually left soon after.

Those departing lads were then faced with the same two options that greet all of us during moments of adversity: 1) they could either quit their plan to become a Royal Marines Commando or 2) they could figure out what went wrong before cracking on with fixing it. Those that opted for the latter were given a positive parting line: they were told what to work on and where they could improve, and were invited to try out again six months down the line. (Today, individuals who don't pass the PRMC are invited to attend a Skills Week, where they join recuits-in-waiting for a taste of what to expect at Lympstone. Together they work on various drills and techniques that might later come into play in training.) Mindset was key, though. Individuals in that position needed to adopt the attitude that they hadn't failed; they just hadn't achieved, and there was nothing to stop them from succeeding next time around if they acted on the advice imparted to them. (I'll discuss the ideas behind maximizing the benefits of defeat in more detail during Phase Ten.)

Every duty or task in Basic Training seemed to land with a subtle lesson. Personal admin duties, where I had to iron my shirts and shine my boots, became an education in maintaining high standards under pressure, rather than just a regiment-wide requirement to look pristine on parade. (We were told that if a soldier failed to care for their personal admin during a war, they tended to physically deteriorate pretty quickly.) Speed-marches across the hills, executed with a heavy bergen rucksack on my back, proved I could exceed any physical limits I'd previously imagined for myself. The motives for pushing us on in that way were obvious to everyone groaning and hurting in their bunks after another day working in the rain and mud. We were pushing past what we thought was possible.

We were being toughened up.

Unsurprisingly, I became used to pain, but I was helped by the fact that everything was being done in bite-sized chunks – *small steps*. Yes, we were getting forced out of our comfort zones, but not in a way that was designed to destroy us. For example, we weren't thrown into nine-mile time trials on day one. Instead, we built up to it, bit by bit. At first glance, our initial physical training sessions resembled a Mr Motivator workout – a series of push-ups, sit-ups and other movements that felt like easy work for the first ten minutes, the whole troop moving as one in white kit and plimsolls. Our casual attitude stopped the following morning when everybody realized they were unable to move without groaning in pain. Before long we were vaulting over the gymnastics box and embarking on periods of Battle Physical Training where we would carry logs across muddy fields and scale assault courses. All of it was considered gradual progress. All of it was bloody agonizing.

The first time I was asked to jump over the gymnastics box, I felt a little intimidated – and confused. *Why am I being asked to do this? It seems a bit silly to me . . .* I thought. My attitude to the task was amplified when an older lad from my troop, in his twenties, made his first attempt. Having launched himself into a pretty powerful run-up, he aborted his jump at the last second (or maybe he forgot what he was supposed to do; I'm really not sure). There was an audible yelp as he slammed into the box and crumpled to the deck. Everyone in the gymnasium either winced in sympathy or laughed as the bloke rolled around on the floor, holding his crotch in agony. It later turned out that the impact had twisted his balls, which was a pretty serious injury and forced him to leave the course a day or so later. I sometimes wonder what type of military career he might have had were it not for that shocker of a training session. But the lesson of the gymnastics box was pretty obvious to anyone watching: *without bravery, failure is inevitable.*

Injuries were par for the course, though. People were constantly twisting their ankles on long runs through the mud, or breaking bones on assault courses. I remember that all of us suffered horrific rashes when training on Woodbury Common in Devon. The area had gained a fair level of notoriety in the Royal Marines because part of the work at Woodbury required the recruits to crawl through vast expanses of gorse, the prickly 'Bastard Bush' that scratched a person to pieces as soon as they touched it. The pain was made worse when the Bastard Bush's victims inevitably fell foul of a horrific condition known as Woodbury Rash, an angry infection that burned and itched for ages.

The results of these unpleasant tests were noticeable. I became a little bit more robust with each step and training soon taught me that my physical and mental breaking points were much higher than I'd previously believed. After around fifteen weeks of work, I felt bigger, stronger, harder to kill. *I'm a bloke now*, I thought. Every step had caused me to grow. I'd learned how to be courageous, and this became increasingly evident on the infamous Tarzan assault course, which included a fourteen-minute dash up cargo netting, along death slides and over a number of other gruelling obstacles on the Bottom Field at Lympstone. It was an intimidating challenge of body and mind that caused an emotional malaise whenever we were about to embark on another run of it, and the troop had fondly nicknamed it 'the Bottom Field Blues' – a feeling of dread at the pain to come. But we did it anyway because we'd built ourselves up to the job. *We were ready.*

The same step-by-step philosophy has also been applied when moulding elite athletes into championship form. Prior to a track and field season, short-distance sprinters endure background training, a physically exhausting period where they run for longer distances than their event, at high intensity. For example, a 100m or 200m racer will run leg-buckling 300m sprints over and over, usually until they're on their hands and knees and puking their guts on to the grass. The idea behind this brutal regimen is that it gives an athlete the strength to run their highest speeds for lengthier periods of time during a race. They develop race endurance and build up power step by step until their standard distance feels comparatively easy.

At first, repetition shows the athletes what they can overcome. But background training, like Royal Marines Commando training, also teaches an individual about their mental and physical limits. A nagging knee pain on the 200m corner might unsettle a runner during their first race of a campaign, but if they've felt it over and over in training they'll recognize the sensation as being temporary rather than season-ending. A coach will often tell his or her athletes to push on in those moments because it allows a competitor to better understand their body in times of stress.

All of us can learn from the step-by-step approach. All too often we fail due to overreaching in the early stages of a project. People arrive at the gym for the very first time and throw their back out because they want to lift heavy weights like an experienced trainer. Start-ups fail because the owner immediately wants to go toe to toe with an established brand and they find themselves floundering in the battle. Had they adopted a step-by-step approach, those individuals would have gradually increased their technique, courage and resilience in the same way that Royal Marines recruits perform a series of stamina-training sessions before attempting the gritty speed-marches. It's also why addicts take one minute, one hour, and one day at a time when recovering from personal behaviour issues. Or why professional footballers begin their league campaigns with pre-season training rather than moving straight into the first game of the season unprepared.

Through training and exposure to stress, bravery can be built up in pretty much the same way. Novice skiers or snowboarders often find the trickier, expert-level black runs intimidating having first spotted them from a chairlift. But by improving their technique on the easier blue and red runs, those same riders are able to build the skills and confidence required to take on the more challenging terrains of a mountain. Similarly, anxious singers, actors and musicians can develop the nerve required to perform in front of crowds by starting out in smaller rooms with friends and then working up to large venues with paying customers.

As the Royal Marines have learned, the considered, step-by-step approach is essential if we're to see long-term progress. But it works in flashpoints, too. Sometimes an event is thrown at us and we feel intimidated. The very thought of taking it on can swamp us to such an extent that we short-circuit, or freak out. As a result, we're unable to manage the pressure and we fail. But the truth is that it's within our power to negotiate the biggest tests, even though we might *feel* as if we're breaking under the weight of a particular challenge. We just have to cut it up into smaller pieces.

One trick I've used to help with that process is to focus on the *here and now*, rather than the bigger picture: I concentrate only on the One Metre Square around me, figuratively speaking. For example, an operator in serious emotional discomfort shouldn't consider the long-term stresses of the battle they're embroiled in or what their teammates are doing. Rather, they should adjust their attention on the immediate metres and seconds around them. *Are they under cover? What are they in contact with? Where do they have to move to next?* Considering what might happen in the wider conflict is too big, too overwhelming, and only intensifies any distress being experienced. But by focusing on the moment, that same operator can function effectively.

I've been on missions where a boat we've been travelling in has capsized during a heavy storm. In the immediate moments after being dunked into the water, it didn't help to fret about the final destination or how quickly we were going to get there – our vessel had been upended. The size of the waves crashing around us was irrelevant, too. Instead, it became vital that I dealt with the issues that were instantly accessible: the stuff I needed to do in order to survive. *Where is the boat? How quickly can I swim to it? Is there anybody around me who's in serious trouble?* I brought those factors into my One Metre Square and dealt with them only, shutting out everything else as best I could.

In many ways, the One Metre Square theory is a method of breaking down a huge body of work into smaller, more manageable chunks; it pulls a very big and scary situation into a tangible space and moment. Handily, it works in a number of contexts. Maybe our challenge is to write a bestselling crime novel. To consider the book as a whole, on day one, with its 100,000 words of text, chapters, characters and storylines, can be a pretty intimidating experience. The thought of deadlines and the workload might cause us to spin out and stall. Instead, we should bring everything we need to get started into the One Metre Square. These might be:

What is my main character like?

Who is the 'big bad' in this story?

What is their conflict?

We do the research. We make the notes. We build the world we're going to write in. Then we can move into the next metre square, concentrating only on what has to be done there and then. *And the next. And the next . . .*

I've found this to be an effective way of focusing my thoughts during a challenging event. The stress quickly recedes into the distance. Often, when looking back, I've been amazed to see how much progress had been made.

The boat has righted itself.

I'm back on the oars.

The crew is dealing with the next massive wave. And the next. And the next . . .

#2 DETERMINATION
NEVER GIVE UP

My determination was challenged every day as a Royal Marines recruit. With every new test of my resolve, the Lympstone instructors pushed me harder.

'Yeah, we're asking you to do something that's fucking hardcore,' they seemed to be saying. 'And the only way you'll be able to finish it is with determination. If you don't have determination then you can fuck off, because nobody's forcing you to be here . . .'

Weirdly, that idea of self-management was inspiring. There was no safety net and it was true: nobody had ordered me to be there, crawling through the muck and the wet as blank rounds and smoke grenades exploded around my head. I was there because I *wanted* to be, and if I dropped out I'd only have myself to blame. Later, that way of thinking continued into Selection, where self-determination was a vital characteristic for anyone hoping to fight at an elite level. There were times when I'd get up at 4 a.m., the rain hammering down outside; I could hear it on the tin roof and windows, and nobody in the group was under any illusions as to the pain and misery awaiting us once we started working. Inevitably, one of the lads would then yawn, roll over and quit.

'Fuck it, I'm not going out.'

The others would cajole him. *Come on, mate, you can't quit now. You've come this far.* But the damage was done. He was finished. As I left him to it, I'd often think along similar lines. *Oh, mate.*

Quitting looks so easy. I could chin it off too. The negativity had become contagious. Then I'd remind myself of my motivations for being there or I'd imagine the spoils of success. That visualization process was enough to ensure my work got done.

I can't remember how many times during those thirty-two weeks of Basic Training I could have walked away. There were days when I was brutalized by the elements. On other occasions, the physical demands required of me were intimidating. We were sometimes ordered to tackle an endurance course of tunnels and pools while wearing Fighting Order – 21lb of equipment plus a 9lb weapon. The experience was horrendous. At other times we executed fireman's carries where we hauled our oppos, plus kit (theirs and ours), across two hundred metres of mud. The clock was running and anyone that failed to beat the required time of ninety seconds was beasted afterwards. On my first attempt I was paired with a mate called Matt who was six foot five and weighed a ton. I picked him up, but my mind wasn't set right. There had been a flash of self-doubt in the build-up and it quickly told. I didn't cross the line in time and the physical training instructor dressed me down: I was 'pathetic'; I'd shown weakness and was letting myself down. The bollocking got to me. I was upset with myself and I definitely didn't want my friends and peers thinking I wasn't up to the job.

I'm not going to pass if I can't get that bloke down the course, I thought.

The possibility that I might not make it as a Royal Marine worried me – I was frightened of failure. My dad had already made one or two snarky comments about my chances and I'd got the distinct impression he doubted whether I could pass the programme. So I used the photograph of him in my room as fuel. I wanted to prove him wrong. I reminded myself of why I'd joined up in the first place and imagined passing out on the parade ground in front of my friends and family. The positive, psychological reframing of my situation helped me not to quit and the next time we gathered at the Bottom Field and had to perform the fireman's carry, I tapped into the bravery already instilled in me during training. I scooped up Matt and flew down the course, crossing the line well ahead of time. The effort bloody hurt, but the results surprised me. From then on, I knew that with determination I could handle anything the Marines threw at me.

As a motivational tool, the visualization of success was one of the most powerful in my armoury.

#3 UNSELFISHNESS
OPPO FIRST, TEAM SECOND,
SELF LAST

As far as I'm concerned, unselfishness is the most important value within the Commando Spirit. The idea of putting your opposite number first – with the team coming second and self last – creates cohesion within a group. In turn, cohesion builds resilience; resilience leads to success. However, the core reason for encouraging an unselfish spirit within the Marines is that it's virtually guaranteed to develop a strong team effort. During battle situations, a considerate attitude is vital for ensuring that missions are completed successfully, with the minimum number of casualties – it's far better to act as a group than a collective of lone wolves. A selfish Commando will only look after themselves and soon becomes a weak link.

A selfless spirit is encouraged within everybody in the Marines from day one. There are the obvious training drills, such as the aforementioned fireman's carry. But there are also other, more subtle techniques that ensure every individual looks out for their team. When I first arrived at training, I was pretty naive about the type of tasks that were required of a functioning adult, let alone one that was hoping to succeed in the military. Domestically, I was useless. Mum had done so much for me while I'd lived at home that even basic house-keeping duties felt daunting. What I hadn't realized when first signing up for the Marines was that I would have to master the art of self-care. Learning to look after my kit and polishing my boots became as important as learning to fire a weapon, but I struggled under the pressure. The stress of executing basic household procedures soon overshadowed all the training and caused me to worry when I should have been focusing elsewhere.

From day one, the recruits were thrown together in six-man rooms where nobody could afford to be selfish. We lived on top of one another; there was no room for privacy. That meant if we wanted a decent night's kip, it was important that the group all chipped in with the domestic tasks that needed to be checked off every day. At sixteen, I was much younger than a lot of people in the troop so the older recruits, who had more domestic experience, had to help me through. I often struggled with ironing, wrestling with my shirts into the early hours until I became frustrated – I couldn't get my head around it and the lack of sleep left me exhausted, which then caused me to suffer during some of the physical tests. Eventually one of the older lads showed me what to do and I found myself on an even keel again. But I made sure to repay that favour whenever I could. If ever I had to pick up my boots from the drying room, I always grabbed everybody else's boots too. During moments when our room had to be cleaned and we were missing a person, I made up for it because to work as a team meant the whole group got to rest up earlier. That recovery period was vital if we were to perform at our best the following morning.

My unselfish attitude extended on to the training ground. Recruits were constantly ordered to keep an eye on the lads working around them. I'd alert somebody if their pocket was open, their bergen wasn't secured properly or they looked like a bag of shit, because if one person screwed up we were all punished. A recruit with an unbuttoned pocket was once called out by the senior trainers and then verbally thrashed in front of the group. As a lesson, he was made to watch as everybody else was then physically beasted around him.

'Right, you dicks,' the instructor would scream. 'Get into the push-up position. The reason you're doing this is because Silly Bollocks here can't get his personal admin straight.'

Nobody grumbled or blamed the person responsible, though. Instead, we took it upon ourselves to become more vigilant. If we wanted to avoid an afternoon of endless push-ups, it helped to keep an eye on the state of our oppos. An admin-related thrashing always served as a stern reminder of our responsibilities.

'Start looking out for each other!' our instructor would conclude. 'Do you understand what we're trying to say? If you're unselfish, this doesn't happen.'

The troop would respond in unison: 'Yes, Staff!'

From then on, everybody would keep a lookout for any unzipped pockets and loose webbing. Silly Bollocks rarely screwed up twice. Meanwhile, the rest of us became even more careful when working through our own personal admin.

Annoyingly, I've since noticed that the idea of unselfishness – oppo first, team second, self last – doesn't really extend into civilian life. Once I'd left the military, I briefly took on one or two corporate jobs as I tried to figure out what the hell I was going to do next. Almost immediately I was shocked by the selfish attitude of some of my co-workers. They skived, got caught and then blamed others for their mistakes. Whenever somebody screwed up, they rarely accepted the consequences of their actions. People seemed happy for others to pick up the slack for their shoddy work effort. It drove me mad. I knew their lazy attitude wouldn't have gone down well with the people I'd served alongside because the military consequences of being self-centred were terrifying, especially in a gunfight. There was much more to be gained by owning up to a mistake made on a British Armed Forces tour, because to have knowledge was to have a tactical advantage. For example, in a stressful situation nobody liked being surprised to find that somebody hadn't mentioned they'd forgotten a piece of equipment or made a procedural error.

If that sense of shared responsibility were to become immediately prevalent in many businesses, teams and organizations, they'd become more successful overnight. Instead, the every-person-for-himself mindset has been allowed to rule the roost and nobody takes care of their oppo. As a result, mistakes creep in, people fail and performance levels diminish. But encouraging an unselfish attitude in the workplace, or in an activity or event where teamwork represents a powerful value, is always a smart move. In any environment, having someone else's back usually means they'll have yours. For example, if an individual offers to 'spot' somebody as they lift weights in the gym, there's a good chance that person will return the favour. Implementing this one facet of the Commando Spirit should help both of them to train even more effectively and they'll both become tougher as a result. Remember: cohesion builds resilience; resilience leads to success.

#4 CHEERFULNESS
IN THE FACE OF ADVERSITY: MAKE
HUMOUR THE HEART OF MORALE

Why look for humour in war? Well, there's no point in whinging when life gets noisy or if a situation turns to shit. It doesn't help an individual or a team if someone starts bellyaching in tough times. One of the reasons the Royal Marines are considered to be one of the most resilient elements of the British Armed Forces is because they've been encouraged to bring positive thought into negative moments. At Lympstone, we were trained to be the Thinking Soldier – a term that's been mentioned regularly on *SAS: Who Dares Wins* as a way to describe what's required of any recruit hoping to cut it at the very top. For the Thinking Soldier there's no room for negative emotion, such as anger or fear. In against-all-odds scenarios he or she speaks positively rather than griping about their fucked-up luck or their mistakes, and gallows humour is often used to ease any tension. They then consider their next steps calmly, executing the plan with confidence.

There's a legendary tale of specialist soldiers in the Falklands War hiding behind a wall in the middle of a section attack as heavy gunfire ripped the sky to shreds above them. Rather than freaking out and rushing into their own deaths during a mad charge, they took a fag break, got a hot drink on and assessed their angle of attack – before taking down the enemy soldiers, firing at them in a considered assault. What would have happened if one of them had started moaning or gone into an emotional tailspin? Fear and pessimism is contagious. The chances of them making it out of that situation would have decreased rapidly if one of the lads had decided that survival was impossible.

This positive mindset was first installed within every Royal Marines recruit during our Basic Training. Humour helped a person to bounce back from adversity or failure because it encouraged them to move on more quickly. When people were struggling with the workload, or we'd been presented with a series of rough tasks, the instructors often made a joke or snarky comment. It was as if they were sending a warning to the troop: 'Right, we're going to be throwing you lot into some pretty hairy situations. Sometimes in those hairy situations, it's going to be pretty dark. You might feel like you're not getting out of it, but you'll need to find some positivity if you're to have any chance of fighting another day.'

Once the hard graft started, that idea was emphasized further. Don't get me wrong: to suggest that the work was light-hearted would be wide of the mark. Instead, jokes were applied when appropriate. If anybody screwed up during Battle Physical Training they were rinsed by the group afterwards and nobody was deemed immune from a piss-taking. When the physical thrashings felt unbearable, it helped to have a laugh about it. I remember being holed up in a ditch on a mock night patrol as the rain hammered down. I was feeling cold and miserable. For a while, I half-wondered whether being a Royal Marines Commando-in-training had been the best career move for me. Unexpectedly, somebody nudged me in the ribs.

'You know, Foxy, civilians pay thousands to do this shit . . .'

'Fuck off, do they.'

The laughing and joking started soon after and I quickly forgot about being soaked through in a muddy hole at 3 a.m.

A positive attitude has also helped me outside war. In 2018, I worked on a Channel Four documentary entitled *Meet the Drug Lords: Inside the Real Narcos*, which required me to meet some pretty intimidating characters in the cocaine badlands of Colombia, Peru and Mexico. There was more than one occasion when I feared getting taken out by a hired assassin. A number of the drug kingpins I met were suspicious of my motives for being there; there was a worry I might be an undercover cop rather than a TV journalist, and I had meetings with masked traffickers where heavy weaponry was always on display. (I was unarmed throughout.)

During one of the heavier moments in the making of the show, I was called to a crime scene where a torso had been dumped in an Acapulco side street. Unsurprisingly, the sight of a hacked-up body was grim, but as we filmed the police officers working around us, a shout went up that we'd been lured into a trap. There was a real risk that the corpse was bait – a trick designed to lure the cops into the open where they'd make an easy target for any waiting narco. I'd brought a friend of mine along for morale, the former-Royal-Marine-sniper-turned-professional-explorer-and-TV-fixer Aldo Kane. We had been mates for years and I trusted Aldo to watch my back as I interviewed some of the most feared individuals in the drug wars. I also knew that Aldo would lift my spirits during some fairly hairy situations. But moments before we were ordered to take cover from a potential sniper's bullet, the pair of us had been arguing over a cigarette lighter.

'Fuck you,' snapped Aldo eventually, storming off to crouch behind a car for protection.

I took shelter by a brick wall. 'Yeah? *Fuck you.*'

Once we'd realized the severity of our situation, the pair of us calmed down and switched on. The argument was soon forgotten. Before long, Aldo and I were laughing like school kids over our silly tiff, which helped to ease the tension of a potentially dangerous situation. There was a chance we might have been in trouble and so any residual animosity or negative thought wasn't going to help us if somebody opened fire on our position. We needed to work as a team; we had to be tight, and humour was the best way to swipe away any animosity between us. It was also another healthy reminder of the lesson I'd first learned at Lympstone: *Always try to look on the bright side of life, because moaning will never help you in a gunfight.* This giggling might have seemed like madness to the film team working alongside us. *But there was a method.*

It has been scientifically proven that optimists live longer. Those odds obviously change when optimists are dropped into the middle of a war, but the mentality required to succeed in such a dangerous environment is drastically improved by a 'glass half full' attitude. In a 2019 study, researchers from Boston University's School of Medicine discovered that people who described themselves as optimists were more likely to live to the age of eighty-five or beyond. It wasn't as if the study relied on a small survey sample, either: over 70,000 people were questioned about their attitudes to living. Their health was tracked afterwards and it turned out that the positive thinkers extended their life span by 11–15 per cent.

'This study has strong public health relevance because it suggests that optimism is one such psychosocial asset that has the potential to extend the human life span,' wrote one of the study's authors, Lewina Lee. 'Interestingly, optimism may be modifiable using relatively simple techniques or therapies.'

The science as to *why* optimism helps us to live a longer life isn't yet clear, but it goes to show that putting a brave face on things can give us all a tactical advantage in tricky situations.

OPERATIONAL DEBRIEF

>> Resilience is best developed in phases, if possible. Start slowly. No heavyweight boxer goes twelve rounds during their first-ever training session. Instead, they build slowly over months and months of preparation, gradually increasing the effort until they're physically and emotionally ready for a bout.

>> Push on through the pain; you might learn something about yourself. A physical twinge or emotional block could be a sign that you've reached your limit, but make an attempt to carry on regardless. The sensation might only be a psychological hurdle, one you're able to smash through. It's always worth testing your breaking points.

>> In a shit situation, think positively. Whinging won't get you anywhere, but positive thoughts reap rewards. Negativity is contagious. Stop it spreading.

>> Visualize the rewards of success. When working through Basic Training I pictured the faces of my friends and family as I passed out as a Royal Marine on the parade ground. During moments in missions when extreme endurance was required, I imagined sitting in a pub in England when the military tour was completed.

SITUATIONAL AWARENESS
THERE'S ALWAYS MORE IN THE TANK

A soldier with situational awareness has a greater understanding of the moving parts around them, such as what their teammates might be doing and the area they're moving into. Mental alertness allows them to spot threats and notice potential escape routes or dangerous obstacles within their immediate environment. A good example of situational awareness in action would be a routine patrol in an urban environment. Is a soldier aware of the approaching pedestrians moving up behind him? What about the fast-moving car turning into the street? If the enemy were to strike at that very moment, where would they move to for cover?

Building an alertness to threat is vital in theatres of conflict: it allows troops to dig themselves out of trouble quickly, plan for troublesome events ahead of time and dissuade the enemy from attack simply by looking battle-primed. In US Marines training, recruits are sent into a woodland environment and given ten minutes to find and mentally note several items hidden in the trees. To simulate the physical exertion of a combat situation, they then have to perform a series of burpees before listing every hidden item they've noticed during the drill.

Installing a sense of alertness and an understanding of our surroundings is vital when building resilience and combat intelligence, so every chapter in *Life Under Fire* will deliver an endnote of situational awareness – a lesson designed to increase your operational capacity while working under pressure, or a tactic or idea for improving resilience levels.

One theory that's naturally instilled by the training in both regular and elite soldiering within the British military is the idea that the body has much more to give, no matter what the brain might be telling you. In reality, the mind is lazy. It wants to give the muscles and major organs a rest in times of physical hardship. But often, while the body might *feel* like it's close to breaking point, the truth is there's often plenty more fuel left in the tank.

One way of shorting that particular mental circuit is to find gratitude in suffering. If that sounds weird, consider the following examples from my time in Basic Training at Lympstone:

The pain of lugging a teammate on the shoulders for two hundred metres can be celebrated: you're still alive.

Any pain or frustration experienced during the Tarzan assault course is an achievement: it means a potential Royal Marines Commando is still in with the chance of passing out at the end of the gruelling thirty-two-week course.

The mind-twisting frustration at having to polish boots to a pristine shine is an opportunity to develop discipline.

Gratitude has long been recognized as a valuable tool when striving for resilience because it stimulates three areas in the brain: 1) The anterior cingulate cortex, which helps us to concentrate and which links our thoughts and emotions; 2) The brain's stem region, which is responsible for producing dopamine, a neurotransmitter that allows us focus, to find drive and to explore; and 3) The striatum, the reward centre, where the dopamine ends up.

When these three areas are working well together, a person becomes happier and more productive; they're also more impervious to the kinds of stress thrown up by intense events, emotional challenges and the difficult workloads I experienced on Royal Marines Basic Training.

In other words, when we're going through the shit, it helps to adjust our thinking. Don't moan about it; be thankful instead. Find gratitude.

While rising at 3 a.m. to power through a tricky work project, remember the trust and respect people have placed in you in order to get the job done.

In the middle of overcoming an illness, be thankful that you'll be able to recover and function again.

In moments of painful physical effort, don't stress about the hard yards ahead; picture the ones you've already completed and feel pleased they're out of the way.

Try to briefly picture the worst-case scenario – failure, frustration or, as in my case, that photo of my old man and his reaction if I flunked – and use it as fuel to drive you on to the end. Then imagine the spoils, focusing on them when the pain threatens to become overwhelming. By allowing the brain to do the heavy lifting, the body will be more inclined to carry you to the end.

PHASE TWO

THE POWER OF PURPOSE

My Royal Marines Basic Training and the Commando Spirit laid the foundations for long-term fortitude. However, to become truly resilient I had to discover my purpose.

Purpose is propellant. It fires us like a bullet towards whatever target we might be aiming for. It brings commitment, bravery and desire, allowing us to break through barriers we might have previously thought impenetrable while forcing us towards our goals. In tough times, purpose can be enough to see us through to the end. If we have a cause to scrap for, then anything is possible.

An extraordinary example of this happened in the United States in 1982 when an American woman, Angela Cavallo, was reported to have saved her son's life after a car had slipped from the jacks he'd been using to support it. In the accident, Cavallo's son was pinned to the floor, but she summoned up an unknown reserve of strength, heaving the car upwards while two friends repositioned the jacks, and pulled him to safety. Physiologically, her superhuman lift had plenty to do with an extreme surge of adrenaline, but purpose – being a mum, saving her kid's life – was the catalyst.

As an example of what can happen when somebody is being powered by purpose, this is about as apt as any. But you can find that drive too. All it takes is a few simple steps.

Life carries momentum for people with a 'why'; having a reason for what they do makes them stronger and resistant to some pretty scary twists of fate. Meanwhile, people without a 'why' can sometimes find themselves feeling restless, isolated and frustrated. At times they can become vulnerable. I know this because I've lived through both sets of circumstances. The strength that comes with having purpose helped me to become a senior operator in the SBS, but I've also endured the emotional stress that kicks in when purpose is stripped away. I've learned that the knack to becoming resilient is to have something to fight for, and that the chosen something is always unique to the individual. It could be a significant other, family, a charitable cause, self-respect or professional success.

The importance of finding your purpose, or 'why', when building resilience isn't a revolutionary or new theory. However, it's one that a lot of people seem to have overlooked. In his 2009 TED Talk 'How Great Leaders Inspire Action', the motivation expert and author Simon Sinek explained how everything should start with the 'why'. In a theory he called the Golden Circle, Sinek listed the 'perspectives' shared by successful companies and leaders. Having drawn three concentric rings on a whiteboard, he wrote the word 'what' in the outer circle (for what a person or company does). The middle circle was the 'how'

(how the person or company does their 'what'). And finally, the inner circle, the bullseye on the target, was the 'why' (the major driving force behind the 'what' and the 'how'). Too many people or companies, argued Sinek, have started with the 'what', when in reality the route to resilient and robust progress is to focus on the 'why'. Sinek explained:

> 'Every single person, every single organization on the planet, knows what they do, 100 per cent. Some know how they do it, whether you call it your differentiated-value proposition or your proprietary process or your USP (unique selling point). But very, very few people, or organizations, know why they do what they do. And by why I don't mean to make a profit. That's a result. It's always a result. By why I mean: What's your purpose? What's your cause? What's your belief? Why does your organization exist? Why do you get out of bed in the morning? And why should anyone care? As a result, the way we think, we act, the way we communicate, is from the outside in.'

In other words, if you start with the 'why' then your chances of success increase considerably.

Sinek then outlined how a tech company like Apple had become so resistant to tricky market forces when their equally competent competitors had failed. He argued that Steve Jobs and his colleagues had focused on a clear 'why' when establishing Apple as a brand. Sinek continued:

> 'Here's how Apple actually communicates: "Everything we do, we believe in challenging the status quo. We believe in thinking differently. The way we challenge the status quo is by making our products

beautifully designed, simple to use and user-friendly. We just happen to make great computers. Want to buy one?"'

Put like that, Apple's 'why' has been pretty compelling so far. But all of us have a 'why' within reach. My personal experience with purpose began with the desire for adventure and self-improvement through the military. It's currently fuelled by the need for self-care and a desire to inspire others who suffer from mental health issues. As Sinek explains, it's vital that everyone begins their next project, career move or lifestyle change with the 'why'. For example, a business developer might open a community farm in response to a local government incentive – let's call them Developer A. Another, Developer B, might have an ambition to connect people in a positive manner or to change the way in which society views food consumption, the environment and the importance of shopping locally, so they, too, might open a community farm. I reckon that in tough times, Developer B will have the motivation to stay the course. They have their own internal purpose. *They've discovered their 'why'.* But Developer A, with their purpose decided for them, has a greater chance of falling away or quitting.

Don't be Developer A.

STEP ONE
FINDING YOUR 'WHY'

Finding the 'why' doesn't always begin with a lightning strike or a once-in-a-lifetime event (though it can definitely happen that way). According to Angela Duckworth, Professor of Psychology at the University of Pennsylvania, author of *Grit: Why Passion and Resilience Are the Secrets to Success* and previously an advisor to the White House and the World Bank, the way a person usually finds their purpose is much more progressive. Having interviewed the Stanford development psychologist Bill Damon, the book suggests that people with a 'why' begin with three steps:

1) They find their 'spark' – an interest, or passion.
2) By watching someone else succeed in a similar way – a 'role model' – that spark later develops into a moment where the person understands how this passion might accomplish results 'on behalf of others', while seeing the emotional rewards it could bring.
3) The person realizes their achievable accomplishments can make a difference in the wider world.

My military career probably followed a similar path to the one outlined by Professor Duckworth. I'd signed up with the Marines as a teenager straight out of school. I wasn't a bad lad when I was growing up in Luton, but lessons bored me to tears and I was often in trouble. It wasn't anything too worrying; I wasn't a violent kid or a bully. In fact, I hated bullies – it's one of the reasons I joined the Royal Marines in the first place. But I couldn't get my head around the work, or exams, and I needed something exciting to grab my attention. I was always hearing stories about the Marines from Dad and I loved mucking about in the outdoors, so I signed up on the Potential Royal Marines Course. *Step one: I'd found my spark.*

Having made it through the training programme, life clicked into place in the Marines. I took signals courses and made trips to the jungle, the Far East and the Mediterranean, but I saw very little in the way of action. The hostilities in Northern Ireland had calmed down and nothing much was going on elsewhere. I eventually became sick to the back teeth of listening to a load of old-timers banging on about the Falklands and the first Iraq war. I wanted more. I needed to push myself to improve. I wanted to be pressurized and to find out if I could cope at the highest level, with the best soldiers in the game, serving the military. After ten years of serving as a Royal Marines Commando, and having heard all the stories about what the Special Forces were doing and what they were achieving for the UK Armed Forces, I applied for Selection. *Step two: Having watched the people around me, I wanted to know if I could achieve the same results, 'on behalf of others', through my passion. I wanted the buzz of being the best of the best.*

I didn't need to worry about a lack of action. Within a few weeks of beginning Selection, I listened enviously as the War on Terror kicked off in Afghanistan. By the sound of it, all my old mates were in the thick of the scrapping, but I didn't care too much because life as an elite soldier would eventually give me more autonomy, more control and more focus (and I'd end up deployed somewhere along the line whether I'd passed Selection or not). I'd also get to do loads of cool stuff, like raiding enemy buildings and fast-roping out of helicopters – all the things a lot of young boys dream of doing as they grow up. Once installed in the conflict as an operator, my mental resources were stressed much further than they had been in the Royal Marines. The fighting was intense and dangerous. Missions took place every night and the schedule was physically exhausting. But all the way through I knew I was doing the right thing. *Step three: My spark and achievable accomplishments were making a difference in the wider world.*

I told myself I was helping my country to defeat a militia force, or forces that wanted to wreak havoc upon innocent communities. I was taking down bad guys and destroying their infrastructure, smashing into terrorist training camps and tracking down IED facilitators. I had a cause, and the personal horrors of war were manageable for me because I saw them as a sacrifice worth making in order to secure the safety of people I loved at home and of the civilians who were being oppressed by unpleasant forces within the countries we were working in. Whenever I had doubts regarding my personal safety, I remembered my 'why'.

My experience of finding that propellant for my career might sound incredibly simple when written down as three steps. But the process I went through is probably familiar to anyone claiming to have found their purpose in life. Those steps, based on the work of Stanford's Bill Damon and Professor Duckworth, are also easily replicated: 1) Find your passion; 2) Watch others accomplishing results 'on behalf of others', while seeing the emotional rewards their efforts bring them; 3) Figure out how you can make a difference in the wider world.

With purpose as fuel, you'll become more resistant to adversity. Say you love trekking and for charity you want to make it to the top of one of the Seven Summits – the seven continents' highest mountains: Aconcagua (South America), Denali (North America), Vinson (Antarctica), Elbrus (Europe), Kilimanjaro (Africa), Everest (Asia) and Carstensz Pyramid (Oceania). The training will be tough and at certain points the effort might threaten to defeat you. But with a charitable cause at your back you'll feel less inclined to quit. And if that cause is one you feel personally connected to and makes a difference to somebody you know and love, you'll feel inspired to push through the pain and finish the job whatever happens.

STEP TWO
THE DANGER OF LOSING PURPOSE

Without purpose we can become vulnerable, as I discovered when my 'why' was suddenly torn away.

By the time I left the military, in 2012, after twenty years of service, I'd been rinsed. My first onset of PTSD had kicked in a couple of years previously while I was working on a night assault, as the three helicopters we were in swooped on to an enemy compound only for us to be attacked by an unexpectedly large mob of gunmen. The intensity of the work, and what I had seen and experienced during the assault, left a devastating mark on me. Day by day, week by week, my enthusiasm for the job waned in the fallout. I couldn't see the point in being an SBS operator any more. The operations that once filled me with excitement were leaving me hollow with dread. *I had lost my purpose.*

I wanted more than anything to get my mojo back, and I tried bloody hard to reclaim it. I spoke to psychiatric nurses at the Royal Marines' base, where I lived and worked while not fighting abroad, hoping they could present me with an armoury of techniques and processes to help me get back on my feet. 'I want to *want* to return to battle,' I told them, but there was nothing they could do. As far as they were concerned, my time was done. I was prescribed anti-depressants, which were like a death sentence for a bloke like me. I became withdrawn and moody with each dose. My experiences and some of the horrors I'd witnessed haunted me like ghosts, especially my memories of traumatized youngsters I'd seen after a gunfight or suicide bomb in a civilian area. At times, I became so spaced out that I struggled to communicate with the people around me.

Previously I'd been in the thick of the laughing and joking when I'd been away on tour with the military. Now I was a shell, retreating into the shadows until I was eventually medically discharged. The job that had once given me a reason to get up in the morning was gone and no pill was going to help me – not fully, because the pain wasn't coming solely from a chemical imbalance in my head. I'd been detached from my sense of purpose through extreme stress, so medication was only a Band-Aid; I'd have to go much deeper emotionally in order to recover. The answer was to find a new purpose, though what I hadn't realized at the time was that it couldn't be forced, or created artificially in a quick fix. It had to be genuine, authentic. Much in the same way that pills couldn't truly replicate a long-lasting and healthier state of mind, so manufacturing a 'why' or striving for a purpose I didn't really believe in would only lead to disappointment.

I know because I tried, and failed.

Bloody hell, starting out in the Real World was tough work. I'd hoped that my first day of civilian life was going to be the first page of the opening chapter in a brand-new book. In reality it was more of the same pain. I was miserable, fuzzy-headed and unable to find any meaning to what I was doing in life. I ended up landing a job as a project manager in a company that special-ized in delivering infrastructure services. It was OK work, but there was nothing to match the excitement of taking down a truck of enemy guerrilla fighters as they opened fire on our pos-itions in a desert stronghold. I was bored out of my brains. Worse, I had lost my sense of self. Stripped of all meaning, life seemed worthless.

That's when I decided to throw myself off a clifftop on the south coast.

At this point in the story, it might sound as if all my resilience had deserted me. I was definitely running on fumes, but I had enough in the tank to drag myself away from the edge, and from the tide smashing on the rocks below. With the support of a couple of friends, I was able to seek help. I came to understand why I'd been ravaged by the emotional stresses of war and why my focus had waned. I was encouraged to live in the 'now', con-centrating on my immediate surroundings rather than dwelling on the mistakes I might have made in the past, and I learned how to manage the fears I was feeling for my future.

After a while, I took these ideas on board. Had I ignored the advice, there's a good chance I wouldn't be writing this now. And while the really hard work was still to come, I soon discovered that I wasn't alone (though my experience was definitely at the extreme end of the spectrum). For many people, a crushing sense of grief can follow the loss of a job or a role in society. At times we all lose steam. We fall out of love with something or someone that once got us out of bed in the morning, or our priorities might change. The trick to surviving, as I was about to discover, was to refocus.

I had to find a new, authentic 'why'.

STEP THREE
RELOAD

Being freaked out by change is never a good thing and during my time as an elite operator I'd been trained to be flexible enough to handle a constantly evolving enemy threat and to work in a number of different environments. During training, specialist soldiers are often flung into a series of changing situations for that very reason.

I remember being part of an exercise where different parts of the armed forces had been positioned all over the country and abroad. Units were located across the UK. The exercise represented a mock mission that was focused on readying us for a terrorist attack. There were eyes on a 'dummy' hostile cell, with a bunch of young Royal Marines playing the enemy. We attacked their base in a drill and my group was then airlifted by helicopter and flown to re-deploy to react to intelligence gleaned from the 'enemy' base. From there we were deliberately pulled from pillar to post: I was part of a group that boarded a Hercules transport plane and flew to another airbase where we had two hours to ditch our scrapping gear for jumping kit. Once we were back on the Herc, we were flown to the coast where we parachuted into the sea before being picked up by a ship and taken to the north of the country. A massive night assault on an island base completed the exercise. The number of moving parts involved was ridiculous, but it provided vital preparation for what was to come in my career, and throughout life generally, where spinning plates and dealing with ever-changing environments and adversaries was a constant challenge.

The rhythm of war had been just as unpredictable. Some days I'd be fast-roping on to a terrorist base; on other occasions I'd find myself walking into a town or village in search of a hostile leader. With every new challenge I'd had to be mentally up for the scrap – *I'd had to be comfortable in feeling uncomfortable* – so I decided that the negative emotions of handling a major life-change, of the type I was experiencing as a former military veteran in therapy and looking for a new 'why', was no different from any unpleasant moment I'd endured in war or in training. The process of getting up and moving forward as I searched for a new purpose wasn't that much of an emotional shift from, say, taking off my dry kit after a night in the jungle (we wore only dry clothes in our bunks) and climbing into my stinking, soaking-wet kit for another day of running around in the heat and humidity.

My first movements to finding a new purpose were slow, but steady. I understood that if I were to reclaim my resilience, I'd need to get back to my old self. I had to find authenticity, and I could only do that by focusing on a fresh objective. With some help I tried to locate a new avenue of work that would give me a similar level of purpose as my old role in the military. One ambition involved me working outdoors in a job where I was able to push myself to the absolute physical limit. The other involved me helping people that had found themselves in a similar set of circumstances to mine.

Over several months, I listened to my gut. I then landed a role rigging up safety lines for a Comic Relief event. That led to a diving job in Madagascar with a film crew, which utilized the skills I'd picked up as a Royal Marine. Having made my own luck by pushing myself in a direction where I was able to thrive, I was approached to appear on the Channel Four show *SAS: Who Dares Wins*, where I could operate in a challenging environment with three other former elite soldiers, sharing a camaraderie similar to the one I had been used to in the military. The show, which featured former operators Matthew 'Ollie' Ollerton, Ant Middleton and, later, Mark 'Billy' Billingham, pushed civilians into some of the challenges forced upon soldiers hoping to make it through Selection and into the Special Forces.

Those new roles gave me my spark, my new passion. I had made it back to Angela Duckworth's step one.

Now that I had a purpose – to help those who were in a similar position to the one I'd been in; to work outdoors, pushing myself to my mental and physical limits – I found confidence and a renewed sense of well-being. I watched other former military lads succeeding in new roles and I became stronger. I was able to challenge myself in new ways by planning expeditions and setting goals that used all the skills I'd learned in the military and allowed me to exercise my passion for adventure. In 2016 I rowed across the Atlantic with Team Essence, a five-man crew comprising former Royal Marine snipers Aldo Kane and Ross Johnson, Royal Air Force copper Mathew Bennett, a mutual friend, Oliver Bailey, and myself in a world-record-setting adventure in which we achieved the fastest unsupported row across the Atlantic, making it from Portugal to Venezuela in fifty days, ten hours and thirty-six minutes. Once that was done, in 2018 I skied across the North Pole for charity.

Those trips weren't only about personal glory, though. *They also represented Angela Duckworth's second step: Having watched the people working around me, on the expeditions and on* SAS: Who Dares Wins, *I wanted to know if I could achieve results, and help others, through my passion.* Through sponsorship drives I raised cash for charities I felt very closely linked to, such as those dealing with the issues of male mental health. Following my experience of PTSD, I realized that helping other lads in a similar mess to the one I'd found myself in was something I wanted to explore further. If I managed to successfully combine that work with an outdoor activity, then I'd find a similar sense of purpose to the one delivered by the military. Of course, the stakes weren't nearly as high, but the rewards and sense of well-being would come close. With a mate of mine, Jamie Sanderson – another former Royal Marines sniper who'd also had his life torn to shreds by PTSD – I set up a community interest company called Rock2Recovery. Our aim: to help trauma-ravaged veterans and their families to find suitable therapists and alternative treatments for some of the psychological wounds caused by conflict and high-stress situations.

In a way, I was creating exactly the type of therapeutic space I'd been crying out for when my own life was falling apart. *Duckworth's step three: Suddenly my achievable accomplishments were making a difference in the wider world again.* One of the very first things Rock2Recovery did when meeting with new faces at our walk-in clinics was to discuss purpose. We talked about finding exciting new challenges for people. These might have been experiences that got the adrenaline racing while delivering a physically and emotionally rewarding response, and some lads I spoke to went on to raise money for charity by running marathons, climbing mountain ranges and cycling amazing distances. We also encouraged people to find a creative outlet in which they could heal themselves. Jamie had become a songwriter and I went on to make TV shows and documentaries; I also wrote the book *Battle Scars*, detailing my experiences with PTSD.

Whenever I've been able to, I've encouraged former military personnel with mental health issues to think about the route I've taken because I am living evidence that locating a new sense of purpose is the first step in pushing the body and mind into places that might previously have seemed impossible. Because without purpose, the battle is already lost. In life we sometimes have to endure situations where unexpected change is thrust upon us and we're forced to find a new purpose. Our partner leaves, we lose our job, illness or injury affects our ability to perform a function we loved. The key to surviving those devastating events in the long term is to unlock a new 'why' in the three steps outlined by Angela Duckworth, steps that are applicable to everyone:

1) What is it that makes you truly happy?
2) How have other people achieved success by using that same process, skill or passion?
3) In what way can your work in this new field achieve results in the wider world?

OPERATIONAL DEBRIEF

》 Purpose is rocket fuel. No matter the challenge ahead, if a sense of importance is attached to the task, any action that takes a person nearer to completing their goal will come with extra motivation. A slog of endless nights in the office is made so much easier if the carrot of promotion is being waved or if the work feels really worthwhile. If those honking sessions of cardio in the gym are needed to prevent a serious health issue, or to achieve a specific goal, finding the motivation required to step on to the treadmill suddenly isn't so difficult. It can work on a purely emotional level too: somebody living through a family tragedy can be strengthened by the knowledge that their staying strong during incredibly challenging circumstances will help the other people around them.

》 Find your spark. *What do you love?* A creative passion, physical activity, charitable endeavours, a business idea or team objectives are all good jumping-off points.

》 Once you have your spark, find ways in which it might achieve results elsewhere. The person using fitness to overcome a serious health issue could use their new-found skills to help their friends to train. The head chef from a failed restaurant might note the mistakes made by their bosses and open a business of their own, making sure to avoid the pitfalls that trapped their former employers.

▶ Try to make your achievements count in 'the wider world'. Once you've achieved that, you've found your reason for getting out of bed in the morning.

SITUATIONAL AWARENESS
HOW TO SURVIVE CHANGE

Some of what we're talking about in this book requires a reframing of thought; to look at a negative or challenging situation in a different light or, in other words, to put a positive spin on an unfolding shitshow. And nowhere is this more applicable than during the tricky process of finding purpose, because this can feel completely overwhelming at times.

By working through therapy, I learned a lesson we could all benefit from: when striving to find a new purpose, it's so important to let go of the old. I didn't chuck my past life away completely. I remembered the mistakes that later became other lessons; I enjoyed talking about the accomplishments and experiences that my time in the military had given me; I felt pride in my old purpose. But I realized it was vital to accept the inevitability of something coming to an end, because whether I liked it or not, nothing lasts for ever. We grow older. We retire. People we love come and go. Our priorities change. Jobs we once enjoyed finish or become irrelevant. When we hit a certain age, we can't play sport or exercise in the way we'd like. To realize that change is unavoidable is a first step in rediscovering purpose during tough times.

Acceptance makes us resilient, but clinging on to the past is self-destructive. I've since seen it in some of the military types I used to work with – retired soldiers mourning for a job they once loved. We all get together every now and then, and the lads who are struggling are easy to spot: they're the ones that haven't accepted that their fighting days have come to an end. All they want to do is talk about the past. They'll look on their time in some pretty ugly situations with fondness and everything they experienced is viewed through rose-tinted glasses. Then they'll make out that the modern military life is 'shit'. Usually, these meet-ups take place in a boozer decorated with war memorabilia, plaques and old photos. It can be bloody depressing.

That type of attitude can be found in just about every walk of life. Sports stars hanging up their kit have a tough time accepting that their identities are changed for good. They miss their old teammates or coaches, even the ones they didn't like that much. Like people in the military, their new day-to-day routines become unrecognizable. The thrill of competition and self-improvement vanishes overnight. Without acceptance, they can struggle to find a new purpose. Without purpose, life can sometimes seem pretty stale. Swap the job titles around and you'll find the same problem everywhere: city workers, business owners, property developers, creatives, people in the emergency services, chefs, even therapists . . . The list is endless, but the problem remains the same. Pining for the good old days makes it impossible to move forward.

Luckily, I came to learn that change *is* possible. My resilience could return with a different purpose. As I began my own recovery, I noticed examples of it everywhere. Mates of mine who had once been hardcore operators were reinventing themselves in the private sector, where they worked successfully in big corporations by applying the same levels of self-discipline and focus that had served them so well in the past. Other blokes I served with decided to set up their own businesses – renovating properties, distilling rum, even producing high-end technical clothing inspired by their military experience. In every case, the work was hard, but the rewards were huge. All of those lads had endured the turbulence that comes with a changing life. All of them came through successfully.

One of the hardest things about finding a new purpose is the overwhelming sense that we're starting from scratch. It's bloody scary. There's pressure to locate a new calling, a life-altering transformation or idea. The very thought of it can freak people out and cause them to quit before they've even started. When speaking to people at Rock2Recovery going through a challenge of this kind, we tend to revert to the step-by-step method used by the Royal Marines in Basic Training: we suggest small forward movements rather than giant leaps of faith.

For example, sometimes it's enough for a person that their new purpose is to *imagine* finding their new purpose. For other people their new purpose might be to take care of themselves for a few weeks with some rest and recuperation at home. That can be enough to get them through until they want to think about locating their next calling. Family, good health and positive friendships are also good jumping-off points for a new purpose. It really doesn't matter what the motivation is, and it can be constantly evolving. The important thing is to make that first move.

PHASE THREE

THE EXPERIENCE FACTOR:
KNOWLEDGE DISPELS FEAR

Experience is everything when it comes to building resilience.

In the military, gruelling periods of training are used to deliver important lessons and each one tells an individual how to function effectively in dangerous situations. There were plenty of times where I was operating in unusual circumstances behind enemy lines – such as during a heavy aerial bombardment from a hostile force – where my training had equipped me with a level of background knowledge and confidence that prevented me from spinning out. My experience told me I could execute the mission.

From the moment work began with the Royal Marines Commandos, I was exposed to a series of physical and psychological tests. Each one was designed to build strength and stamina, but they also presented me with an internal hard drive of experiences and memories. I jumped through assault courses and crawled through tunnels and ice-cold rivers so that real-life combat wouldn't seem so physically confusing. I completed battle drills with blank rounds and smoke grenades. When the bullets and bombs flew around for real, my head told me, 'I've been in a similar situation before. I can handle this.'

Everyone can become more robust through experience; we only have to push ourselves. In the military elite, I was given the opportunity to grow through learning, sometimes in unexpected ways, which I'll detail over the coming pages. The logistics of what I did will probably seem extreme, but the principles behind the work I undertook are applicable to anybody . . .

The British Forces shove a lifetime of experience at their troops during training, for one simple reason: it keeps them alive. It's well documented that the hard work done away from the extremes of war can adequately prepare an army for the stresses to come. Soldiers become more robust; armies increase their performance levels; conflicts are won as a result. But the ways in which experience is imparted are as important as the whys. It's not enough simply to throw a person in the deep end – sometimes literally, expecting them to adapt and survive immediately.

According to a commonly used but uncredited theory, there are four positions, or 'zones', of experience a person has to work through when building resilience:

1) The Comfort Zone. Here a person is protected by familiarity. It could be the less-than-challenging job they've been doing for years, the uninspiring exercise routine they fall back on or the same old predictable patterns of behaviour. Life's pretty cosy here, but there's no real progress or personal development.

2) The Fear Zone. Escaping the Comfort Zone for the Fear Zone is probably the toughest step because the Fear Zone is an area of self-doubt and insecurity where any imagined challenges or hopes a person might have had for themselves are greeted with a chorus of doubting internal noise. *A promotion? You're having a laugh, mate! A 5K? No way!* Here begins a battle of self-confidence where the strong-willed push through but the weaker person finds an excuse to bail and returns to the Comfort Zone.

3) The Learning Zone. Life gets pretty interesting if a person can move past their discomforts, beyond fear, to the Learning Zone. This is where new skills are developed and hurdles are overcome. As a result, a person becomes stronger and is now able to thrive in challenges that might previously have crushed them.

4) The Growth Zone. Having picked up a series of new skills within the Learning Zone, the individual finds they are suddenly stronger, more experienced and increasingly capable as a result. From here on they're able to hit whatever targets they might have originally set for themselves and plan new goals for the future. In essence, their new comfort zone has expanded.

These principles are well known and widely used, and I've witnessed their effectiveness during the training of soldiers in the British Armed Forces. I stepped through all four zones as I progressed from a scrawny Royal Marines recruit into a battle-tested operator. But I've seen how this process works in business, too: companies preparing for major change – such as a digital overhaul – have to leave the Comfort Zone and enter the Fear Zone, then gain experience in the Learning Zone, before reaping rewards in the Growth Zone. Individually, we work through these same steps in a number of situations, from learning to drive to starting a family. In order to grow from a nervous, first-time house buyer into someone capable of buying an investment property, a person has only to work through the four stages of experience, though the biggest challenge is undoubtedly taking that first, nerve-wracking step away from the easy life.

THE COMFORT ZONE
BREAKING FREE

As I mentioned earlier, our brains like to give us an easy ride, and often the mind decides we're exhausted when there's actually plenty more to give. Rather than tackling the early-morning gym session, the inner voice convinces us to stay in bed. Instead of facing up to our problems, or having a difficult conversation with a significant other, we procrastinate, believing that tomorrow will give us a better opportunity at change. We're locked into the Comfort Zone and breaking free of it can be tricky.

I identify with this process because it pretty much mirrors my decade with the Royal Marines. Any peacetime soldier comes to realize that there are only so many training exercises one can do before they become routine. I found myself feeling comfortable and safe, *too safe*, especially once the training had familiarized me with some of the physical hardships of military life. Every now and then a new challenge would arise and I'd get nervous again, such as when I first learned to abseil, but the excitement was fleeting. To summarize: my life as a Marine was bloody good fun, but in the absence of real action I felt too cosy in the job, with fewer and fewer opportunities to test and expand my knowledge.

Looking to push myself, in 2001 I applied for Selection. At the time the 9/11 attacks on the USA were a few months away so the War on Terror had yet to take off. Don't misunderstand me: I've never wished for war. But in the same way that fire-fighters hope to attend infernos, soldiers want to work in their field of expertise, applying their skills where it really counts. I was making that first step towards the Fear Zone.

But I wasn't really prepared.

I knew about the challenges of Selection. Conducted over six months, twice a year (in the summer and winter), the process first served up a gruelling Aptitude Phase, which took place in the hills of the Brecon Beacons, an unforgiving mountain range in Wales. The work was known by everybody to be bloody challenging and I was placed on the winter Hills Phase, which kicked off at the beginning of January. Following a heavy Christmas, I was a little off the pace and soon paid for my time in the Comfort Zone as a group of hopefuls ran up and down a series of mountains, weighed down with heavy equipment, in a succession of long yomps. After a while, the Hills Phase became doable though still difficult. But what really put me into an area that most people would consider the Fear Zone was a challenge I couldn't prepare for, an alien and hostile environment. Succeeding in this unknown place – and we all fear the unknown – would later help me to make it into the military elite.

It was time to face the jungle.

THE FEAR ZONE
FINDING THE MINERALS

The Fear Zone is probably the most important phase when building resilience through experience. Overcoming obstacles within it can lay the foundations for any major changes to come, but it's an experience, or challenge, that feels utterly miserable in the moment. It might require a ruthless period of honesty (admitting to an emotional problem), some serious self-discipline (early-morning training) or a painful sacrifice or two (quitting the cigarettes and fry-ups). But afterwards, in the glow of achievement, the rewards become apparent. The feel-good endorphins experienced at the Fear Zone's end are long-lasting and sometimes life-changing. In the aftermath of such an event, it's not uncommon to experience a boost in confidence, a psychological transformation or an altered worldview.

The jungle was definitely my Fear Zone.

From the minute I walked into it, its ecosystem was on the attack. Almost immediately we were introduced to the 'Wait-a-while Tree' – which we also called the 'Bastard Tree' – a tangle of razor-sharp barbs that tore at my clothes and flesh whenever I was unlucky enough to walk into one. Moving too quickly sometimes resulted in serious injury, so the best technique for escape was to 'wait a while' and calmly pick off the hooks one by one rather than trying to wriggle free. Not everybody has the patience for that. Over the years, a number of lads have been CASEVAC-ed from the jungle, having been carved to ribbons by thorns.

The Bastard Tree wasn't our only natural adversary. When

setting up camp, our first job was to look for deadfall – branches or large tree limbs with the potential to come crashing down during the night. Testing for loose wood became one small part of a never-ending war with Mother Nature. The humidity was intense; it was very difficult to breathe. Within seconds of leaving the helicopter and moving under the vast canopy of tropical rainforest – which resembled an endless sea of broccoli as we flew towards it – I was soaked through with sweat.

The wildlife was just as dangerous. I was actually helicoptered out of the jungle following a scorpion sting that turned nasty. Insect bites were a way of life when living under the trees, and for the most part I dealt with scorpion stings pretty well. When a scorpion struck it felt as if a searing-hot needle had lanced the flesh. The most painful one happened when one of the bastards crawled into my trousers and stung me on the ball bag. It was agonizing. At first I didn't know what had happened, but when I tore my trousers down I spotted a black shape with an all-too-familiar stinger tail scuttling away. My knackers burned for hours.

The most important thing when dealing with insect bites in the jungle was to protect the wound from infection afterwards. Bacteria thrive in humidity and damp, and all the lads had pots of iodine stashed in their first aid kits. Whenever there was a break in the exercises, everybody tended to their cuts and grazes. Scratches on the knees or elbows were the worst. Once those areas were infected, the joint often became so inflamed it was almost impossible to function. Ankle wounds were pretty bad, too, as I found out to my cost when a scorpion crawled into my boot one day. It jabbed me as I moved, and keeping the cut clean afterwards was impossible.

The hole in my flesh rubbed against the inside of my boots and all sorts of dirt seeped into the skin. The infection soon climbed up my leg and, having picked up a blood condition, I became delirious. A medic hooked me to two drips as I was flown to hospital, where I remained bedbound for a week.

For fuck's sake, I thought. *Why is this happening to me? Maybe this isn't meant to be . . .* I wallowed in self-pity. For a while I convinced myself that my military ambitions might be beyond me.

But then I remembered I'd been holding my own within an environment that was considered to be the ultimate test of modern soldiering and I focused on my purpose again: *I wanted to join the elite.* I was later told that the cut would have been impossible to keep clean and that the instructors, or Directing Staff (DS), were surprised I had lasted as long as I had with that injury. That was all the encouragement I needed.

I told myself I'd been given a test run and that I would return stronger than ever. *Maybe my extraction had been a blessing in disguise?* I'd certainly be more prepared and ready to stay on top of my personal admin in situations where basic soldiering was vitally important. I took the fact that the injury hadn't taken place in a life-or-death situation, such as a war zone, as a positive. Training was the place to make mistakes, after all. Before long the change in my thinking meant I was keen to get back into the thick of the action, no matter how horrible it was set to be. *I had overcome the thankfully brief lack of self-confidence I'd found in the Fear Zone.*

These days I apply a similar thought process to any negative incident that might happen in my life. I accept the fuck-up – whether it's my fault or a situation out of my control – draw the lessons from it, leave the rest of it behind and move on. I later learned that this was the only way to function during conflict. Negativity is contagious in terrifying situations. A fearful attitude on the battlefield is often the difference between death and walking away to fight another day.

Some other experiences in the jungle were equally horrible. During one patrol, when it was my time to rest, I fell asleep against a tree. When I woke up, I could feel something swollen in my mouth. Even worse, *it was wriggling*. I poked around my tongue and gums with my finger until I'd found the culprit. A tiger leech had crawled into my gob and was blood-feasting on the inside of my lip. The beasts were attracted to carbon dioxide and I'd often see them crawling towards me, homing in on my breath as I hid in the undergrowth. I pulled out a can of military-grade mosquito repellent and squirted it inside my mouth until the leech let go and I could spit it out, leaving it to wriggle away to find another victim.

New and gruelling experiences were thrown at me over and over and over again. We performed CASEVAC drills where we carried our teammates through the foliage for hours; there were intense live-firing exercises and patrols. At any time we might find ourselves being bumped by a mock enemy, so we'd have to move into action without warning. It was without doubt some of the hardest work I've had to do outside a war zone.

Much of the difficulty when functioning at an elite level was the mastery of personal admin. Because of the wet and the heat, self-care was even more important than usual. Without it, equipment failed, but given the conditions, looking after my kit felt like a never-ending battle. The jungle soon became a vital lesson in the importance of taking care of the smallest details. There was shit and muck everywhere under the trees, which then found its way into every nook and cranny of my bergen rucksack and boots, and I was having to constantly clean and check my equipment. The DS would announce an inspection whenever the mood took them.

'Right, I want to see everything out of your bergen,' a trainer would yell. 'I want to see it all!'

Our weapons were then checked to make sure they were clean and functioning; the magazines were looked over for dirt. My machete was regularly assessed for rust. Even my toothbrush and Steritabs (water-sterilizing tablets) were looked at. The DS wanted to know that we were taking care of our personal hygiene, too, because to fall apart physically was a failure. Getting foot- or crotch-rot was inevitable if an operator didn't wash properly, and the pain was debilitating.

The lessons regarding those small details, though seemingly minor in the grand scheme of things, would help me through war and, later, as a civilian. While living in the jungle, I realized doing even the basics well was vital when operating in a war zone because a poorly cleaned weapon might jam when I least expected it. Later, when preparing for the filming trip for *Meet the Drug Lords: Inside the Real Narcos*, and conducting an expedition across the North Pole, I knew that ignoring personal admin was likely to bite me on the arse at a critical moment. I had to be hyper-vigilant about the small details at all times because surviving under extreme pressure often hinged upon my mastering the mundane, as it did in any expedition role or work scenario.

The type of challenges found in the Fear Zone soon came into play. The DS would deliberately conjure up situations to seed self-doubt and insecurity. I knew that no matter where I was, or what I was doing, one of them would be lurking in the trees, watching and taking notes. The thought was unsettling; at any moment they might want to check my weapon-handling skills or they might notice that my safety catch was on while moving towards the shooting range. At one stage I was leading my patrol during a contact drill where we'd have to engage with enemy targets. As point man, it was vital that I was the first to spot any potential hostiles, but suddenly I heard a shout behind me: 'Contact left!' I'd missed a target and as the firing started, I knew I'd screwed up. Once the drill was over, I took a beasting.

'What the fuck were you doing there?' said the DS. 'As point man you're supposed to be fucking aware! You're a fucking idiot, missing that target, Fox . . .'

The DS sighed. 'You've let yourself down there,' he said disappointedly.

You've let yourself down there. The dig put me into a spin for a while. I worried that I'd screwed up any chances of progressing. I worried that the other lads were stronger and more effective than me. But after a while I settled myself down. I knew the DS had deliberately planted a mind bomb and they were probably watching to see if I would unravel in its aftermath. They wanted to know if I could bounce back from failure and learn from the lessons; they were testing my emotional resilience. I quickly pushed the blunder to the back of my mind; I knew that experiencing self-doubt was an understandable reaction to the circumstances I was in. Rather than letting the criticism weigh me down, I told myself to learn from the mistake, to try my best not to repeat the fuck-up and to push ahead. After all, dwelling on negativity, such as the doubting voices in my head, would only increase my chances of failure. I shrugged them off and cracked on. It was a vital learning moment.

In the Fear Zone I also realized that comparing my performance to the efforts of others was pointless. I had to focus on myself and the task ahead of me, not the struggles and successes of the people elsewhere in the group. (I deal with this subject in more detail in Phase Six.) Meanwhile, ignoring the doubting voices around me, especially the casual remarks of the DS – which were designed to put me into a spin – was vital when trying to execute the job in hand. There was no room for pessimism or negativity in extreme circumstances.

With those processes in place, I finished my time in the jungle far stronger than when I'd begun. From then on, I knew I had the skills and resilience to progress into the military elite.

I could manage just about anything. *The jungle had been my Fear Zone* – though psychologically that environment could be swapped for any life-altering situation: the intimidating task of setting up a new business (swap out the tiger leeches and Bastard Trees for financial challenges and supply-chain issues); breaking off a toxic relationship (with self-doubt and insecurity questioning your decisions); making a scary first step into unknown territory, such as moving house or taking up a new training regime. All of those events are as mentally daunting as any jungle. But if we can jump out of the Comfort Zone with a willingness to adapt, learn and survive, while withstanding plenty of hard knocks along the way, then we're set up for a period of growth and newfound resilience as a result.

THE LEARNING ZONE
WORKING AT THE SHARP END

I was through the Fear Zone and into the Learning Zone, ready to develop new skills, overcome any hurdles in my path and enjoy a newer, more dangerous Comfort Zone. Not that it was easy. Having passed into the SBS, I was chucked into the deep end from the off and there was no adjustment period. On my first day, having been welcomed and congratulated by my new teammates, I was loaded up with responsibilities and any failure to execute them successfully was met with scorn from the lads around me. Though the introductory period was daunting at first, I soon lapped it up. The challenges I'd overcome within the Fear Zone told me I could cope and I soon began to enjoy my life in the Learning Zone.

At every opportunity I was encouraged to build on my portfolio of experience, often in some quite unexpected ways. I learned about demolition: the subtle art of using just enough high explosive to achieve your aim. There were modules on body-guarding and surveillance. I even went out to the middle of nowhere in Wales and spent a few days learning chainsaw skills. It seemed crazy at first, but each course added new techniques and thought processes. The training was adrenalized, but at all times I was expected to perform at the highest level and quickly while under pressure. The learning environment was intense, with an unspoken rule that I was now serving at the military's sharpest point. *I had to be the best at everything.* One of the phrases that kept getting bounced around was 'the unrelenting pursuit of excellence'. I seemed to be chasing it at every turn, but having come through the Fear Zone of the jungle, I became stronger and more effective.

I loved the autonomy within the Learning Zone, as understood by the British military. Being a specialist operator, I was never screamed at. Nobody ordered me to manage my kit in a certain way or to function in a certain style. Whenever I was given a task, I was expected to execute it with a minimum of fuss. If new equipment was being installed, I had to learn how to utilize it in the best way possible. With nobody to kick my arse, I was forced to motivate myself, and it encouraged me to adapt and improve using the resilient mindset that had been developed by Selection. The DS had looked for people who were naturally self-reliant in stressful situations and could learn under pressure. They needed to become comfortable in uncomfortable positions; those situations would enable them to grow. And if they screwed up, they needed to own those mistakes, learn from them and move forward.

While these processes might sound extreme, my experience of stepping up in a new squadron was no different from what a lot of people might expect to go through when joining a new team or taking on a tough challenge. There are new faces to meet and new responsibilities or techniques to master. The first few weeks or months in an unfamiliar situation might seem daunting. There might even be times where we look back fondly at the Comfort Zone, even though we felt bored and stale in a life or circumstances that offered us very little in the way of challenges or hope. But before too long, those feelings fade. We become more confident and capable and we begin to advance in different ways, emboldened by the experience of learning new skills.

THE GROWTH ZONE
ADAPT, LEARN, SURVIVE

It's in the Growth Zone that an individual sees results. It's where purpose becomes focused, objectives are ticked off and new goals are established. In my case, I'd come through some of the hardest military training in the world, and overcome my fears, to learn and develop alongside a group of elite operators. I was now able to put into practice all the experience I'd gleaned and the skills I'd picked up, and, as a result, anything seemed possible.

Working with the elite encouraged me to grow. I found purpose, I set new goals, I conquered objectives. As they say at the RAF training unit Airborne Delivery Wing: 'Knowledge dispels fear.' And nowhere was this more evident than in the SBS, where different training challenges were thrown at an individual to see if they could cope with the relentless rhythm of elite service. Sometimes I would go on diving drills; on other occasions I'd have to operate in the mountains or in Arctic conditions. With each set-up, an individual operator was faced with a series of tasks, each one designed to reflect a potential incident in a real-life war zone.

Our training prepared me and my teammates for the worst of scenarios. We learned skills that would enable us to survive in the most hostile of environments. This wouldn't just be a jungle full of Bastard Trees; there would be mock enemy forces searching for us too. The experience was stressful and unnerving, but with each scenario and training session I was given a broader picture of what I could expect when I was really in the shit in a hostile environment. Every test told me I could handle a horrible reality. If I was captured, I could stay calm. If I became pinned down by enemy fire while my teammates died around me, I would find a way out. *Knowledge had dispelled fear.* Experience had given me the mental tools to grow and become more resilient.

By my first tour of duty, I was approaching my work without worry or insecurity. I had mental flexibility. *My Comfort Zone was so much bigger than it had been a year or two previously.* Thanks to the operations I'd completed in the Learning Zone, I knew that if an op went south it wouldn't be completely disastrous because I'd been given an idea of how to manage the worst-case scenarios. Sure, the work was almost overly comprehensive, but it meant that every individual was prepared. I later learned that the military wasn't alone in operating in this way. A lot of companies and institutions like to give background training for events that might happen in the future, even if they seem unlikely at the time. Some businesses have pushed their staff through media training should they be asked to face TV cameras or a press conference. Others have armed their workers with emergency-situation training, legal courses or first aid experience. Certain camera crews are even taught how to survive kidnap in a dangerous environment.

The likelihood of workers having to lean upon those skills might seem slim at the time, but the fact that they are trained up means an individual can feel more confident should trouble arise. They are emboldened. And when being pushed into a tricky situation, any past experiences – even if they're abstract – can help a person pull through with confidence.

OPERATIONAL DEBRIEF

» Recognize when you're stuck in the Comfort Zone. If you're feeling bored, uninspired or lethargic, it might be time to change things up. Moving forward doesn't require a person to learn in extremes: we don't all have to live in a jungle for several weeks on end. To become tested again, sometimes it's enough to learn a new skill, apply for a challenging job or push yourself that little bit further in something you're already doing.

» We pick up new skills in the Fear Zone, no matter what work or challenge we're doing. Those techniques are translated into experience and can prove to us that we're able to escape our familiar routines and grow in different ways. By successfully operating in the jungle, I learned to function at an elite level in unfamiliar and highly uncomfortable surroundings. That gave me the confidence to progress, even though some of the skills I'd picked up under the trees were never used again – not directly, anyway (I don't recall having to endure another scorpion sting to the bollocks).

» When working through an unfamiliar challenge in the Fear Zone, try to drown out self-doubt and inse-curity with positive thoughts. Pessimism isn't widely regarded as a useful tool during a crisis. Instead, give yourself a pat on the back for trying something new, focus on the minutes ahead and the immediate challenge in play, and act positively.

》 Once safely removed from the Fear Zone, an individual can expect to pick up new skills in the Learning Zone while becoming increasingly comfortable in uncomfortable situations. If circumstances change in your work or personal life, it's likely you'll be required to master new processes and integrate into a very different system from the one you were previously familiar with. It's OK to feel a little unsettled. Tell yourself that you'll soon learn the required skills and benefit from the rewards later on.

》 The Growth Zone is a phase of exciting results. You'll smash through your preconceived limitations and become more resilient as a result. Depending on your personality type, you might find yourself setting new goals too. Try not to become stale: you might want to escape the new, bigger and bolder Comfort Zone more quickly than expected.

SITUATIONAL AWARENESS

BECOME THE SWISS ARMY KNIFE

As an elite soldier, I was well trained in combat operations, but it was also my job to learn all manner of extra skills that would assist me in the theatre of battle – some of them directly, others indirectly. Once I'd reached the top level in the Royal Marines, it became clear I was being turned into a Swiss Army knife, a multifunctional operator capable of working effectively in all sorts of situations.

I was placed on a wide variety of specialist courses and I became so skilled in one particular field that I was asked to present a talk on my work to the former prime minister David Cameron during one VIP visit.

Once in the thick of the action, no matter where I was or what I was doing, I drew on all manner of experience to get myself out of sticky situations. The knowledge I'd been provided with gave me the confidence to push on even when my work was becoming incredibly complicated. The same attitude towards learning can be used to build resilience.

It's all too easy to stay in one particular lane, to follow the path we've always travelled. However, when unexpected problems come our way, we're sometimes required to think and act differently. That's when the extra skills we've picked up elsewhere in life can come into play. The gruelling training we might have endured during a sport or physical activity – rock climbing or boxing, for example – teaches us about the emotional endurance required to handle a personal tragedy. The boxer already knows how to breathe through pain and stress, while the mountain climber understands how to make considered decisions under serious pressure.

Meanwhile, the dedication needed to learn a language, or stick to a nutrition plan, gives us an insight into the processes required to succeed in another project or challenge. Most importantly, any successes we might have achieved in our extracurricular work bring belief. Some of the recruits who have appeared on *SAS:*

Who Dares Wins over the years went on to overcome personal challenges of their own. Their attitudes towards life changed as a direct result of some of the tasks they were asked to perform for the TV series. The achievement of working through the toughest tests devised by the show made them more resistant to the psychological problems dragging them down in their real lives, and their confidence soared as a result.

The same can happen for you. Take up a new challenge. Master a new activity. Travel somewhere unusual or unexpected. Learn a new skill, one that's very different from your regular line of work. You'll soon escape the Comfort Zone and develop enough added qualifications to become a human Swiss Army knife.

PHASE FOUR

FINDING YOUR TRIBE

With the Commando Spirit's encouragement of 'oppo first, team second, self last', I was taught about the importance of teamwork and alliance. It got me through some pretty rough times. However, once I was entered into combat with the Special Forces, that philosophy became turbocharged and I was indoctrinated into a brotherhood where I had the back of every operator around me, and they had mine.

As the fighting intensified, I was required to operate behind enemy lines, where my work became increasingly dangerous. But I was calmed by the knowledge that everybody within my group was highly skilled, motivated and willing to take a bullet for me if necessary – as I was for them. The operators around me were my tribe. Their assistance helped me to stay resilient in terrifying gun battles; their support encouraged me during missions where I might have struggled had I been facing the same challenges alone.

Unity made me stronger as an operator. The Brotherhood gave me confidence and a belief that I would always succeed in battle, and among the group there was an empathy and understanding regarding the chaotic lives we were leading. A healthy competition between the lads involved also made everybody that much tougher. As a result, I was able to push myself harder, move further away from my comfort zone and grow.

I don't think I was even that close to some of the lads fighting alongside me, but that never mattered. Simply knowing I was backed up by my teammates provided me with an extra layer of reassurance, like a security blanket. We were a team, we had shared purpose and that drove us forward. But nowhere was that unity required more than in one of the most dangerous aspects of Special Forces life, a role where everybody's mental resilience was pushed to the absolute limit . . .

They called us Door Kickers. Elite operators tasked with booting our way into the homes of militia leaders, wanted killers and all-round bad people, our weapons poised, the adrenaline spiking. The job was officially known as a 'hard arrest' and we were often tasked with securing a prized asset, such as an individual or a store of weapons. In terms of risky jobs, being a Door Kicker had to be up there with the worst of them because nobody really knew what to expect on the other side of the entrance. Still, it wasn't uncommon to receive a shock or two. Sometimes those surprises were pleasant, amusing even. On other occasions, they resulted in extreme violence.

The best operations happened when we'd burst into a compound to find our target tucked up in bed, sleeping soundly. On other missions a building was stormed aggressively, my team primed to receive some pretty fierce resistance upon arrival; having entered the building, we were greeted with a room full of chickens. During one infamous hard arrest I heard about, a unit crept up on the desert-town home where a highly prized target was hiding. They steadied themselves for the always-stressful bundle into a darkened building; the fear that a waiting gunman might have heard them as they gathered outside was high. And then the point man leaned forward, accidentally pressing an unseen button set back in the wall. Everybody froze as a doorbell tinkled inside.

'Bloody hell, mate – what have you done?' whispered one of the lads.

There was a split second's pause. The door opened and the target naively shouted out a friendly 'Hello?' God knows what he'd been expecting, but the bloke seemed totally bemused when armed operators piled on top of him. He was quickly restrained. The point man – who was visibly thankful for not getting everybody killed with his epic blunder – was immediately nicknamed 'Ding Dong'. His rinsing lasted the whole tour. Within the SBS Brotherhood it was important to make light of the chaos going on around us, just as it had been during my time with the Royal Marines.

Those were the happy endings. The awful hard-arrest jobs lived even longer in the memory. During one assault, a friend of mine was shot as we burst through the door. The injury looked horrific, but there was no time to check on his well-being because, as a highly trained operator, I had to focus on the job in hand. The unit stepped over his body, engaging our attacker before calling in medical assistance. Luckily he survived. During other raids, I've burst through doors and taken down targets only to encounter the family of a terrorist leader, or bystanders, caught up in the chaos. The relief in holding fire during those situations was always huge.

In situations of that kind it was vital that I acted calmly and in a calculated manner because all sorts of things could go wrong, especially when people were waving weapons around. The potential for rash decisions was high, but I was used to over-coming panic, as was everyone within the Brotherhood. Throughout my career I'd been embroiled in gunfights in confined spaces where civilians were nearby; we'd hunted high-value targets and rescued kids from burning buildings at the same time. It was terrifying work. But my role would have felt even scarier had I been surrounded by emotionally driven or sloppy individuals. (We'll discuss the process of controlling negative emotions in Phase Eight.)

Sometimes I've worked with sketchy recruits in *SAS: Who Dares Wins*, individuals with anger management issues or problems with authority and instruction. Impulsive people might last for an episode or two because they make for good telly, but when assessing their progress afterwards, Ollie, Billy, Ant and I have generally arrived at the same conclusion: *that person wouldn't have made it past the first two weeks had they been on Selection.* Staying calm and maintaining focus on missions was vital.

Having the Brotherhood around me was a huge factor in rationalizing various flashpoints of hardcore violence. Nobody in the military elite enjoyed killing enemy fighters or traumatizing civilians in the fallout, but it was a part of our job in the same way that police officers are sometimes called upon to use weapons when taking down a terrorist or an armed assailant. Unfortunately, their actions often impact any innocent bystanders caught up in the chaos, as did ours. For individuals involved in work of that kind – whether in the military or armed-police response units – the support and respect of their colleagues is vital. In the SBS it helped in processing what was a stressful part of the job, and there was a constant gallows humour that eased the emotional pressure. It also helped that there was a shared sense of empathy for the danger and incredibly brutal situations we were all enduring.

When protected by the understanding and support of my military brotherhood, hard-arrest raids became manageable procedures, if still stressful. It was only once I'd been forced to deal with my demons alone that those same experiences caused me to crumble. Later, when everything had slowed down at home and I was ensconced within the safety net of civilian life, the faces of innocent witnesses soon came back to haunt me. In a team I was emotionally strong. Alone, I'd become vulnerable. I lived with the awful memories for years afterwards.

There was more to the Brotherhood than psychological support, though. It was integral to the very process of Door-Kicking because without it an individual, or team, might die. As a result, every part of the entry process became rooted in unity. When preparing to storm a building, nobody spoke; there was complete silence. To communicate we squeezed the shoulder of the person ahead, instructing them to move forward or to hold. (You'll have seen the process in a load of war movies and TV shows.)

Then we'd commit.

When the group entered, we alerted each other to what was ahead. Often, buildings felt like mazes, strange concertinas of corridors and rooms with very little in the way of planning. The concept of 'flow', as made popular by TV shows such as *Grand Designs*, hadn't been introduced to the regions we'd worked in. The pressure was high, the risks were huge, and the only way to successfully execute a hard-arrest operation was to function as a team.

The process was emotionally charged too. Anyone who said they didn't feel anything during a Door-Kicking job was probably lying. Was I scared, or worried about getting hurt, in those moments? A little bit, but my thinking was usually more positively tuned. I felt empowered *because I was an elite operator*. I brimmed with confidence *because I was part of a brotherhood that was respected and world-renowned*. I felt strong *because I was surrounded by equally committed and highly skilled people*. I'd stand at a door, waiting to burst in with other operators who I knew well. Even though what I was about to do was considered incredibly dangerous, I'd suddenly experience a weird love for the job and for the camaraderie bound up within it.

Among the Brotherhood I'd found resilience. And it enabled me to be even braver and more switched on during moments of chaos.

When highlighting the value of a brotherhood (or sisterhood, or a mixed group, it's all the same, but for the purpose of this book I'll refer to it as 'brotherhood'), it's important to remember that many professions lean in to the concept of resilience through alliance. In jobs where danger is an occupational hazard, such as the emergency services or the military, solidarity is key. But during any team effort, cohesion must be a given if success is to follow on afterwards. Even within situations where individualism is encouraged, there's often a group of people working behind the scenes to ensure that everything functions effectively. It's unlikely Lewis Hamilton could drive so fearlessly without Mercedes' impressive team of mechanics, technicians and designers. Could a world-famous actor such as Leonardo DiCaprio perform so effectively without a collective of agents, managers, scriptwriters and directors around him? Not a chance.

Any emotional issues are also usually dealt with more effectively with a supportive counsel. For support in grief, we often turn to the people moved by the same tragedy, or those who have experienced similar losses in the past. During pregnancies, families-to-be bond with those friends who have already gone through childbirth, and they find new communities and groups to grow with. All of these scenarios encourage the development of a brotherhood in some shape or form. The individuals willing to embrace their new group will often thrive. Those who turn away from it and press on alone can suffer as a consequence.

To the big question, then: How can we create a sense of brotherhood in what we do and then amplify our resilience as a result? In my own line of work, the Royal Marines training at Lympstone forced me first to embrace the idea of becoming a team player. (Oppo first, team second, self last, as discussed in Phase One.) In the military elite, however, the connections between everybody were intensified because the work was so risky. Nothing brought people together quite like a near-death experience. Luckily, everybody who made it through Selection was already well versed in teamwork because selflessness was a trait the assessors looked for in potential operators.

The basics of building resilience through teamwork are absolutely universal, however. After ten years of working at the sharp end of war, I had learned about the power of a brotherhood and the value of building positive solidarity with others. To successfully forge these bonds an individual needs to develop several assets: trust, friendship (or lack of), professionalism and humility – the cornerstones of any team setting.

#1 TRUST

Creating a sense of trust was vital when instilling unity within elite military squadrons. Without it, operators were unable to rely upon one another and missions failed. Meanwhile, a trusting team was more likely to overcome adversity and emerge victorious, because they had confidence in one another.

In that regard, the people I fought alongside understood the importance of honesty. If an operator made a mistake, they 'fessed up straight away and faced the consequences. If somebody promised they were going to do something, they delivered – even at the lowest level, where cleaning the equipment cage or making a round of teas in the mess was a task expected of all. Individuals who didn't follow up on a promise to take on one of those jobs were beasted by the group. This happened for one simple reason: if an operator couldn't do as they'd promised on the base, how could they be relied upon to deliver in a gun battle?

Meanwhile, anyone caught lying to the lads during a military tour – whether that was a little white lie or an episode of barefaced bullshitting – could expect serious retribution in return. Dishonesty pissed the Brotherhood off and our justice was often swift and ugly. Unpleasant forfeits were dished out as penalties. Some lads had to endure having a hot spoon pressed into their flesh. Others had all their hair cut off. The punishments were mostly delivered with a laugh, but there was a serious message beneath the joking: *no one lies*. A strong sense of trust meant the Brotherhood could perform effectively, confident in the knowledge that everybody within it was working as they should.

That attitude helped me to perform, even when I was under serious pressure or scared. Whenever I was point man during an operation, I felt confident that my blind spots were being covered by the lads around me. Later in life, that same attitude prevailed while working on *SAS: Who Dares Wins*, where I've sometimes been tested to the limit. For example, in Series Five, Ant, Ollie and I were asked to perform a backwards dive, in unison, from a ten-metre-high platform into the icy waters of a Scottish loch. The test was in place to ask every recruit still standing a question: *Are you going to be there for the person next to you?* Three candidates had to do it as a team, and if one person bottled it, they all failed.

In the run-up to filming, the specifications for the makeshift diving board had been sent in to the production crew. Along the way, somebody messed up; the ledge was positioned two metres higher than it should have been. While that might not sound like too big a deal, it was actually quite dangerous. A lot could go wrong in those two extra metres and there was a very real chance that one of us might over-rotate and experience a very nasty face-plant on the loch's surface. As it was being built, Ollie, Ant and I looked up at the platform hesitantly. None of us had ever done a synchronized backwards dive before. If one of us choked at the last second, the shot would be ruined and we'd all have to do it again. Weirdly, we were being placed under the exact same stresses as the recruits. There was no time for rehearsals; the tide would soon be going out so everything had to be nailed in one take and there was very little room for error or second-guessing. The mood was bleak at first. I knew it would take a little inner grit to push past the fear. Eventually, we gathered our thoughts.

Fuck it, let's do it.

When it came to filming the jump, I closed myself off. I didn't talk to anyone. I used fear to sharpen my focus as I prepared for the task ahead. Some of the production crew thought I was being a moody bastard, but in reality I was trying to get my head straight. I didn't want to bail, I wanted to be there for Ollie and Ant because, at the critical moment, I knew they were going to be there for me. *There was trust.* The brotherhood within the show would help me to take the leap, and in many ways it wasn't too dissimilar to a hostage-rescue job, where I knew the blokes around me were going to execute their tasks, regardless of any fears they might have.

It worked. The three of us stepped to the edge and folded our arms. Ant spoke into the camera and delivered his pre-agreed cue line: 'You will all turn around . . . and simply *fall*.' And I tipped backwards, knowing the three of us were simultaneously in motion; everybody committed to action together, because it was the only way we knew how to function.

My trust in the others had allowed me to push past my fear.

Direct Action

When looking to build trust with the people you're operating alongside, offer to take on an unpleasant or tricky task. It will show those around you that you're not a person who thinks selfishly. The act will instil a sense of trust and prove to everyone that you can be relied upon in ugly situations.

An example of this is a 'Bottle Tester', a challenge established to check the mettle of any recruits hoping to make it through. The one that sticks in my mind the most involved a diving board and a bell. We were asked to take a running leap off the highest board in a swimming pool; as we leapt, we had to strike a bell suspended from the ceiling with our hand. To make it even harder, the test was conducted in the dark. The experience was terrifying. Nobody wanted to do it, but we all understood the consequences of failure. Not only would the DS have looked negatively upon anyone wimping out, but the growing brotherhood within the team would have been unimpressed too.

The lads who were unable to pass the Bottle Tester were usually kicked off the course, because failing to execute the challenge showed you didn't have the courage to commit – an essential quality in all military training, and especially so when entering the Special Forces. Likewise the 'Battle Swimming Test', where everyone involved had to jump from the high board into the swimming pool wearing webbing, 20lb of Fighting Order and a weapon. Once in the drink, everyone had to tread water for five minutes and then swim for two hundred metres. The examination was concluded with the successful removal of all kit and weapon without touching the sides, before handing everything to the assessor. It was horrible – people lost their shit doing it – but if a person couldn't pass, they weren't allowed to progress. The military had lost a lot of personnel on D-Day when inexperienced soldiers had run off their landing crafts and drowned. The Battle Swimming Test was a prerequisite for entry.

To build trust within your group, find the equivalent of a Bottle Tester and execute it yourself. *Take one for the team.* Sacrifice a weekend so that a shared project can reach its successful conclusion. Maybe accept the responsibility of a major organizational effort, even though the workload will be painfully high. Whatever it might be, your efforts will build trust as a result. They'll say loudly to teammates: *I'm going to be there for the people around me, no matter what.* Your whole group will become even more resilient as a result. In the end, every individual will be more willing to take on unpleasant tasks for the greater good of the team.

That's the theory anyway. But what happens in real life when someone isn't willing enough to step up for the team or a project? As in the Special Forces, showing the courage to commit is vital in any group setting; it builds a sense of brotherhood and strengthens the unit. But if someone in the workplace or team isn't up for showing the same levels of commitment as everybody else, it's imperative to discuss their reluctance. If it's an issue that can be worked on, or worked around, then great. An individual that's unable to operate on weekends because of family commitments or a health issue, for example, might find they're able to pick up the slack somewhere else in the group effort. In this case you can work *with* them. But if the motives are bound up in laziness or indifference, it might be an idea to replace that individual with someone more willing.

#2 FRIENDSHIP (OR LACK OF)

There were plenty of people serving in the job that I wasn't particularly keen on. Lads I'd have hidden from had they walked into the pub: annoying bastards; weirdos; bad apples. That attitude changed in the middle of a gunfight, though. When the rounds started zipping about, I wouldn't have swapped those annoying bastards, weirdos and bad apples for anybody else because I knew I could rely on them to do what was required – and they could rely on me. It was an unwritten code of trust between us, and one that was stitched into the fabric of everything we did. Friendship counted for nothing, at least not in the same way as it did in civilian life. Instead, everybody in a job like mine signed up to an attitude. *The group was more important than the individual.* And everyone I knew would have laid their lives down to save the people around them. That might sound weird to anyone unfamiliar with such a set-up, but it's what kept all of us going in tough times, and such an extreme sense of loyalty is almost impossible to replicate in civilian life.

And that's the real reason soldiers miss gunfights when they're away from war.

The author and filmmaker Sebastian Junger explained this during his 2014 TED Talk entitled 'Why Veterans Miss War'.

In 2010 he'd made the documentary *Restrepo* alongside the British photojournalist Tim Hetherington – the film was a harrowing glimpse at life within the US Second Platoon, Battle Company, where American troops were tasked with defending an outpost in the Korangal Valley in eastern Afghanistan. The outpost had been named after Private First Class Juan Sebastián Restrepo, a medic who was killed there earlier in the war, and the footage is bleak. The assault on the outpost is unrelenting. During the fighting one soldier is killed and the impact on his teammates makes for distressing viewing. But Junger revealed that all of the blokes within the Second Platoon would have happily returned to Restrepo. Not because they enjoyed the violence, but because they valued the sense of brotherhood distilled there. Junger explained:

> 'Some of the [troops from Restrepo] got out of the Army and had tremendous psychological problems when they got home. Some of them stayed in the Army and were more or less OK, psychologically. I was particularly close to a guy named Brendan O'Byrne. I had a dinner party one night. I invited him and he started talking with a woman, one of my friends, and she knew how bad it had been out there and she said, "Brendan, is there anything at all that you miss about being out in Afghanistan, about the war?" And he thought about it for quite a long time, and finally he said, "Ma'am, I miss almost all of it." And he's one of the most traumatized people I've seen from that war.
>
> 'What is he talking about? He's not a psychopath. He doesn't miss killing people. He's not crazy. He doesn't miss getting shot at and

seeing his friends get killed. What is it that he misses? We have to answer that. If we're going to stop war, we have to answer that question.

'I think what he missed is brotherhood. He missed, in some ways, the opposite of killing. What he missed was connection to the other men he was with.

'Now, brotherhood is different from friendship. Friendship happens in society, obviously. The more you like someone, the more you'd be willing to do for them. Brotherhood has nothing to do with how you feel about the other person. It's a mutual agreement in a group that you will put the welfare of the group – you will put the safety of everyone in the group – above your own. In effect, you're saying, "I love these other people more than I love myself."'

That was certainly my experience, and it's hard to accurately describe the sensations that a brotherhood of that kind can create. Physically, I found there was always a fuzzy sensation around me, as if a force field had enveloped my body. Emotionally there was trust. I understood that everybody in my unit was the best in the business, and that also gave me a life-affirming boost. The fact that I was considered their equal confirmed I knew what I was doing, too. That realization gave me a surge in confidence. On raids we often felt like a hunting party, albeit a hunting party on the trail of heavily armed prey. But when it came to enhancing resilience, the alliance we shared in the elite forces felt like an extra layer of bulletproof armour. And nobody cared if they didn't really like the person they were walking behind as they prepared for hostile action.

Direct Action

I've stated that an extreme sense of loyalty, regardless of friendship, is almost impossible to replicate in civilian life, but that's because the stakes aren't usually as high outside of war. Intense experiences – such as gunfights – create intense connections between the individuals living them. In less intense situations, the bonds aren't as strong, but that doesn't mean they can't exist to a degree. And let's face it: we all have to rely on or work with others who we don't connect with very well on a personal level.

The trick to creating unspoken loyalties with those people is to view the bigger picture. *What's our shared objective?* There are countless stories of successful partnerships where the individuals involved haven't got on but they still worked towards a common goal. I know of players within successful ice hockey or basketball teams who have hated one another but still managed to win trophies. Creative forces in amazing bands have travelled in separate tour buses because they didn't see eye to eye, but they still sold out stadium shows and recorded platinum-selling albums. It's also common to hear stories about actors falling out on set, but the film they were working on then won an Oscar or broke a box-office record or three.

In those examples, the individuals involved kept the complaining and arguing to a minimum, coming together to work hard when necessary. *So why can't you do the same?* When moving towards an objective with others, you should certainly get stuck in with the people you like, but invest as much time, if not more, building a relationship with the people you *don't* click with. In these trickier cases, put your personal differences aside and locate a common motivation within the group for being successful. That shared sense of purpose will help to reach your goals and locate group resilience more effectively. In essence, it's the 'mutual agreement' uncovered by Sebastian Junger in the making of *Restrepo*. But instead of keeping one another alive, your motivation might be improved reputation, better pay or the satisfaction of seeing a seemingly impossible challenge through to the end.

#3 PROFESSIONALISM

Once I'd left the Royal Marines Commandos and moved into the more expert SBS, the levels of performance expected were seriously high, and failure to deliver was treated with brutal remarks. I remember messing up on my first couple of days of dive training. We were scaling up and down the side of a boat and I spun on a ladder, the tide pulling me this way and that.

'Get your shit together, Foxy,' hissed a bloke as he passed on the rungs.

I had no idea who it was; the dude was wearing a face mask. But it showed me, in no uncertain terms, that there was no room for failure or scrappy work, even during week one. The zero-tolerance policy for any shoddy performance had a positive effect, though. I had to be professional, and I soon fell into line as I constantly strived for self-improvement. The pressure on me was always high, as it was for everyone, but it was a good pressure. As a result, I and the individual operators around me upped our game. Day by day, week by week, tour by tour, the group became stronger.

That progress brought a buzz. The military wing I'd worked to get into was small and select; everybody knew everybody and there was nowhere to hide. Some lads might have moved around from unit to unit, but generally there was a much tighter weave between us than there had been in the Marines. For the most part the group felt like home, and it was great to see progress, either as a team or in certain individuals. All the operators felt proud of their squadrons, and while there wasn't any specific competition or rivalry between the different groups within the military elite, there was a desire to be considered the very best – unofficially, at least. Whenever a squadron executed a mission in particularly dangerous or challenging circumstances, a sense of pride followed soon after – for those directly involved and every-one else associated with the job. I suppose it was a healthy way of pushing the limits in a very unhealthy occupation.

The high standards expected within the Brotherhood soon helped me to push beyond any boundaries I'd previously im-agined for myself. I became more confident within the group. At times I felt fearless. I was able to perform tasks that might have seemed impossible previously because I was being inspired by the people around me, by blokes I respected and trusted implicitly, operators who appeared superhuman. Driven on by this sense of elite professionalism, I became even more resilient. I executed missions that seem unbelievable to me now, a lot of them involving feats of nerve. I remember feeling nervous about certain parachute jumps; edgy. But as I looked around at the other lads gathering their 'chutes together, my mindset changed.

This is awesome, I thought.

And then I'd remember.

Bloody hell. We're awesome.

My fear seemed to dissipate. And why wouldn't it? I was surrounded by the very best. *I was protected.*

Direct Action

Put your ego aside for the sake of the group. It's easy to become jealous of the successes and results of our teammates within a brotherhood, but negative thought of that kind rarely produces a positive response. Rather than getting caught up in petty rivalries with our colleagues and peers, revel in their success. See their professionalism as a reflection upon your own work and use it as the fuel to drive you on to a better operational ethic.

All too many recruits on *SAS: Who Dares Wins* have allowed their ego to be their undoing. One individual – we'll call them Civilian X – seemed unable to shake their obsession with becoming number one. They tried too hard in all the wrong areas. Whenever a member of us Directing Staff gave instructions to the group, this particular individual would stand alongside us rather than with the team they were working with, and it wasn't long before that person was thrashed for their behaviour.

Civilian X acted as if their shit didn't stink. I suspected that this person was considered the top dog in their profession and wasn't used to being ordered around. Their bad attitude rubbed us up the wrong way; we couldn't wait to bin them off.

But even in failure there was no humility. Most recruits, having been dropped, show disappointment, but it's always displayed with a modicum of respect for the DS. Instead, Civilian X was shocked by our decision. Having heard the news, this individual became defensive.

'What?' they said. 'Why?'

And that was exactly the type of response that had resulted in their removal in the first place. Their attitude wasn't helping the group and wasn't in line with the way we worked in the military elite. When Ant later went in to talk to Civilian X, he offered some consolatory words.

'Good effort out there,' he said. 'Don't feel down about it . . .'

'Yeah, but it wasn't good enough, was it?' said Civilian X. There followed a moaning rant in which the other recruits still in place were criticized.

In the military elite, those with attitudes like the one displayed by Civilian X rarely last for long. Individuals who act in that way simply don't make the grade. Those individuals who do make it through with an ego, or some other emotional issue, are often shaped by the humour and self-policing within the group they eventually join up with. For example, I had a bit of a temper for a while when working as an operator. The reaction of people around me soon helped to keep me in check. I was later nicknamed 'Flash Foxy' and it became a reminder to relax a little if ever my emotions started to flare up.

When working towards resilience, use a sense of competition and a feeling of pride as fuel. Allow these to drive you on to your goals with quiet strength, humility and purpose. But keep the ego at bay – always.

#4 HUMILITY

One of the great selling points when joining the military elite was the looseness of the hierarchy. Yes, there was a rigid chain of command; there were certain people you had to jump to, no matter what you were doing or where you were doing it. And there were a number of procedures and protocols that had to be obeyed by everybody. (It wasn't like a *Jack Ryan* or *Jason Bourne* drama, where operators 'go dark' whenever they feel like it.) But specialist operators were given a far greater degree of autonomy than they were as regular Marines. As I've mentioned elsewhere, no one screamed at anybody when they made a mistake – not like they did in the Commandos, anyway. Elite soldiers weren't expected to stick rigidly to a plan, either. Instead, we were encouraged to think on our feet, especially when operations went wrong. It was then up to us to execute a Plan B as best we could. We were referred to as 'the Thinking Soldier' for a reason.

Why was that autonomous attitude important within the Brotherhood? Well, in a leadership sense it created the idea that everybody was equal. *There was an atmosphere of humility among the whole group.* Nobody pulled rank. The more experienced lads expected to be treated the same as everybody else and preferential treatment was unimaginable. That attitude created a more resilient position because each working unit contained a group of leaders. Sure, within squadrons there were always senior figures; individual units had to be fronted by a team leader. But there was a flexibility within those smaller groups that wasn't present in the regular military, where rank and authority were rigid and everyone else fell in behind. Within the elite forces, operators were built to be both leaders and team-orientated. That way, if the senior figure in a team was killed during an operation, another person could step in and take charge immediately without any drama.

This attitude also helped with planning and debriefing. In those situations, everybody's opinions and ideas were given equal weighting because each individual had a different perspective on an enemy operation during a gun battle. A newer face in the group might notice something in an intelligence report that the more senior heads had overlooked, and that one scrap of information might prove vital.

Meanwhile, egotists didn't do very well in the military elite. Given that the stakes were always so high, there was very little room for anyone giving it the big 'I am', and new operators who had a superior attitude were usually cut down to size when joining up with their squadron. Humility would be forced upon them by the group from the minute they walked through the door, usually through a barrage of piss-taking – if the gruelling nature of the training hadn't thrashed it out of them already, that is.

This process was valuable for one reason: in a war zone, there was zero room for those individuals wanting to play the boss or hero. Instead, humility, equality and a willingness to listen to every voice in the group ensured a strong team ethic was in place. And a strong team ethic led to greater chances of success.

Direct Action

We should listen to everyone working around us. It's easy for senior figures to think they know best, but another angle or opinion on a situation can bring extra intelligence. Meanwhile, a lofty or superior attitude among senior figures in a team can create resentment and mistrust. It's a far better tactic to adopt a humble, but still professional, position.

OPERATIONAL DEBRIEF

» A brotherhood is a key factor in building resilience. The majority of resilient people have a support network of people around them, some of them obvious, others unseen.

» A brotherhood doesn't have to be based upon friendship. Shared purpose is the glue that holds most teams together.

» As with the Commando Spirit, humour and positivity are vital when building a brotherhood. Negativity and defeatist thought is a destructive force within any group.

» In the military elite, hierarchy sometimes takes a back seat to different ideas and opinions. A strong brotherhood will listen to the knowledge and intel from *all* its members.

» A successful brotherhood is one where the achievements and successes of any individual members are celebrated by all. Competition should be used to raise the standards within a group rather than to create division. Put ego to one side.

SITUATIONAL AWARENESS
BUILDING A BROTHERHOOD

So much of what I achieved in the military was a result of being part of a brotherhood. It gave me strength and self-belief. If I could start a business with the lads I used to serve alongside, we'd probably be unstoppable. As a tool for building resilience in war, unity was both robust and multifunctional. I know because I relied upon it during some pretty dark times.

Since overcoming my issues, I've used purpose and experience to get me into a good spot, but I've also built a resilient team around me. Those people now represent a safety blanket during turbulent times and my current brotherhood includes the team from *SAS: Who Dares Wins*, dudes I've worked with during expeditions and creative projects, friends and colleagues from Rock2Recovery, even mates from the gym. My new collective is varied. It's constantly changing, too. Most importantly, it's always there when I need to call upon it.

One of the biggest mistakes I made after being discharged from the military in 2012 was to turn my back on the Brotherhood. At the time, I hadn't realized its importance. Because so much of the support its members provided was intangible, I underestimated the positive effect they'd had on me during some pretty heavy times. Embarrassed at being diagnosed with PTSD, I turned my back on them. I hid away. I didn't call anyone to talk and I didn't ask for help because I worried the Brotherhood might look down on me. Their rejection would have been crushing.

But I should have done exactly the opposite. *I should have got in touch*. My military family was ideally placed to offer advice and support, and during that time I learned a lesson that would change my attitude towards brotherhood for ever: in order to become resilient, it's vital to have a team around you.

For the team players among us, this is easy work. But even the most individualistic of characters requires a like-minded other. Need ideas for locating one? Join a team. Involve yourself in a community project. Become active in new ways and with people you might not ordinarily mix with. Link up with a support group, or with people online. No matter what challenges you currently face or how isolated you might think you are, there are a number of ways to find a new tribe. At the very least, a brotherhood will push you towards your goal. But it might just save your life at some point, too.

PHASE FIVE

SUPERMEN AND WONDER WOMEN: UNDERSTANDING THE TRUTHS REGARDING MEN, WOMEN AND RESILIENCE

Before we get stuck into the next pillar of resilience, I'd like to talk about gender.

When Channel Four first announced that women would be competing on SAS: Who Dares Wins *I felt a little unsure. Not because the idea seemed off the mark – it wasn't and I've had zero problems with mixing the sexes for the show. As far as I'm concerned, mental strength and resilience aren't gender-based and women can be just as tough as blokes.*

My biggest issue with bringing women into the project was the actual foundations of SAS: Who Dares Wins. *The programme was supposed to be a fair and accurate representation of life on Selection, but at that time women had only been invited to apply to the UK Special Forces and as yet none of them had made it through.*

That's not to say the introduction of women hasn't been a success. It has made for some great telly and some of the female recruits have been strong enough to push on to the very end, outpacing many of their male counterparts. As a result, more and more women have applied to be on the show over the last couple of years.

Meanwhile, I was able to make several observations as to the strengths and weaknesses in men and women when operating at physical and mental extremes during filming, on and off camera. They tended to operate in very different ways but had the potential to be equally robust. Understanding those differences and how to manage them is the key to building resilience in mixed-gender scenarios.

Forget the battle of the sexes: everyone has the potential to be physically and emotionally resilient. In just about every gym in the country, you'll find plenty of women with the stamina to run over the Brecon Beacons in a time trial or survive 'the Sickener' on *SAS: Who Dares Wins*; blokes too. (The Sickener is a gruelling test of endurance in which contestants are ordered to perform a series of exercises, such as push-ups, sit-ups and load carries, until a specific number of individuals have dropped out through exhaustion.) At the same time, I know plenty of men who are a bag of shit under pressure and women who wilt at the first sign of a challenge. It had always annoyed me that some people attributed these strengths and weaknesses to specific sexes, and I've become sick to death of people saying that women are harder than men, and vice versa. Those gags about man flu and blokes being unable to cope with minor illnesses feel outdated these days; likewise the comments about blokes acting 'like girls' whenever they're unable to show bravery or physical strength.

That thinking was proved right when the first season of *SAS: Who Dares Wins* to include recruits from both sexes was aired. The men and women working through our challenges were equally resilient and since then we've included women in every season, in both the celebrity and the civilian versions. On a couple of occasions, women have passed through the final tests. Meanwhile, any argument that men are far tougher than women is quickly ended when looking at one of the most gruelling biological processes a female may go through in life: childbirth. As a father myself, it blows my mind that a woman can endure such an incredibly painful and unsettling experience and yet will often want to repeat it. For nine months of pregnancy, the anxiety must be incredible. I've often likened it to some of the missions I've been on, flying into a scrap worried there's a *possibility* I could get hurt or even die. The thing with pregnancy and childbirth is this: women know it's extremely likely they're going to be in pain. And yet they seem happy to put themselves through it to become mothers.

Some scientists believe that women are even genetically more robust than blokes. Certainly, the Canadian-born author, physician and rare-diseases specialist Dr Sharon Moalem thinks so. In 2016, he and his wife, Anna, were involved in a nasty car accident in Toronto. Both suffered nearly identical injuries and were hospitalized for over a month, but Anna recovered more quickly than he did – two weeks sooner, in fact. In Dr Moalem's book, *The Better Half: On the Genetic Superiority of Women*, he points to a number of historical events in which females have shown superior levels of resilience. In a 2020 interview in the *Sunday Times*, Dr Moalem said that one of these episodes took place in the early 1930s during the Soviet Ukraine famine. Millions died, but more women than men survived. Elsewhere, Dr Moalem points out that women live longer than men and they have a higher rate of survival when it comes to diseases such as cancer. They also do better over long-distance sports events such as ultramarathons. In the same *Sunday Times* interview, Dr Moalem argued:

> *'The further the race, the more difficult the conditions, and that's when men start dropping off. Jasmin Paris [a thirty-five-year-old vet] broke the course record by twelve hours [for the Montane Spine Race along the 268-mile Pennine Way, from Derbyshire to Scotland]. At the rest stations along the way, she was pumping breast milk for her baby while the men were flat out on the floor . . . One reason [for women's success in these events] is that women have a lower resting metabolic rate, so they don't exhaust themselves as easily. The other piece of this puzzle that I looked at was famine survival, for which women have an immense advantage. I think that's where the ultra-endurance performance comes from.'*

This idea was also suggested by a 2017 study into the differences between men and women in moments of historical hardship, such as the Irish potato famine and the Iceland measles epidemic, which both took place in the nineteenth century. Entitled 'Women Live Longer Than Men Even During Severe Famines and Epidemics', the report claimed that, while there was no direct evidence of why women are 'life-expectancy champions' in such extreme moments in history – because environment and behaviour also played a role – an examination of infant mortality did point to an interesting biological advantage in female babies: they outlived the boys. Nonetheless, in all the events under investigation in the study, women outlived men too. Having disregarded environmental and behavioural factors with infants, the study used biology as its main determining factor. (According to the report, behavioural disparities in babies were minimal, and the kids would have experienced fairly similar environments, regardless of gender.) Among the theories argued by the study's authors was that oestrogen was known to protect the immune system, while testosterone had the potential to suppress it.

Elsewhere, one other suggestion for females being better at extreme endurance challenges has referred to slow-twitch muscle fibres, of which women have a greater distribution. These muscle fibres use oxygen for fuel, they fire slowly and for long periods of time, delivering steady energy, which is why they're great for ultramarathon runners, such as Jasmin Paris. The scientific feeling is that women are simply genetically better at dealing with fatigue, which helps when competing in ultramarathon-style events.

So, if durability isn't an issue, what's to stop women from making it into the British military elite? I think a lot of the uncertainty when debating whether or not to introduce women has everything to do with the behavioural nuances that sometimes take place between the genders – the kind that can cause problems on both sides. For example, one of the toughest things about working together on an observation post is the intimacy shared by the operators on watch. Being stuck in a hole for weeks on end, surveilling an enemy compound in secret, is rough enough, regardless of who you're stuck next to. But if someone needs to take a shit, there's no option to pop off for a cosy sit-down with a book and a roll of quilted loo paper. The awful reality is that we have to drop our trousers there and then, and crap into a sheet of cling film. We then wrap it up and pop the mess into a bag, just in case any tracker dogs are sniffing around nearby. It's a grim business.

The concern is that such processes might cause issues when men and women are together. As a case in point, during Series Four of *SAS: Who Dares Wins*, one male recruit bailed on the first morning because he wasn't able to share a toilet with a member of the opposite sex on religious grounds. Sure, there are plenty of people that would argue they couldn't care less about those daily events, but the chance that such an issue just might cause a problem has to be taken seriously. When working at the highest and riskiest level, the difference between success and failure often comes down to the tiniest percentage. The slightest distraction – such as a moment of awkwardness between two people of the opposite sex – could lead to failure. However, with a little preparation and management there are ways these distractions can be overcome, as I'll explain later in this chapter.

Channel Four did their best to recreate some of the smaller intimacies experienced by elite operators. The men and women shared living quarters with one another; the men fought women in some of the boxing sessions. But it wasn't the same. That's not to say the process wasn't educational in any way. Some men dealt with the situation well, others failed. Some women rose to the challenge, others struggled. Meanwhile, it became clear that there was definitely gender equality in mental resilience. Most of the blokes were physically stronger than their female oppos, as you would expect, but when summoning the courage to jump into a frozen lake or to abseil down the face of a dam, gender didn't come into play at all.

Interestingly, it became obvious very quickly that the two gender groups on the show were resilient in very different ways. I'll run through them here, but note: I've drawn these observations only from my own experiences on *SAS: Who Dares Wins* – just in case anyone decides to beast me on social media with any accusations of sexism.

GENDER AND EMOTIONAL CONTROL

Let's start with some science.

It's been suggested that the reactions to extreme stress can highlight the emotional differences between genders. In 2015, a research study conducted by the University of Basel theorized that women react more strongly than men to negative imagery; this followed previous evidence that women displayed more facial and motor reactions than men in response to negative emotional images. 'One possible explanation would be that women might be better prepared to physically react to negative stimuli than males,' said Dr Annette Milnik, one of the study's authors. 'Another explanation would be from normative expectations, with women being expected to be more emotional, and also to express more emotions.'

That might help to explain some of what happened in Series

Five when we introduced 'the Marksmen Test', a trial of wits designed to see which recruits could function most effectively and calmly under extreme pressure. The rules of engagement were fairly straightforward. On the night before the event, we informed those eighteen or so individuals still standing (roughly half were men, half were women) that they were now functioning on Card Alpha – a combat situation in which armed forces were allowed to engage in violence if they believed their lives, or the lives of others, were being threatened. The following day we took them to a firing range and performed a series of drills with a blank-firing AK-47. We then thrashed them in the hills with several endurance sessions so that everything they'd learned with the weapon quickly faded from memory. But as the work came to a close, the recruits were dragged to a nearby hill, before individually being pushed, pulled and hooded on their way to a tunnel. They became disorientated. Each recruit was a little panicked.

Which was where the fun began.

A smoke grenade exploded nearby. I let off a few rounds with the AK-47 and the barking sound of gunfire roared around the tunnel. Billy then yelled into their faces.

'We're under attack! What are you going to do? *What the fuck are you going to do?*'

The hood was ripped off and the recruit was then shoved towards the darkness. Each time, the individual involved appeared visibly shocked, but our psychological assault was only the warm-up. At the other end of the tunnel, a man then jumped into view. He was running towards the recruit with an assault rifle, shouting and screaming. Another AK-47 was then handed over to the recruit.

'*What are you going to do?*

'*What the fuck are you going to do?*'

In combat, this was a scenario that required icy calm. The individual running up the tunnel towards the recruit wasn't yet confirmed as a threat under the Card Alpha rules of engagement, nor was his weapon raised, and an operator could only fire if they believed their life, or the lives of others, was under threat. In this case, the person running up the tunnel was a friendly force. As he approached, the Canadian flag on his uniform became visible in the gloom, but on the first occasion that the Marksmen Test was incorporated, all but one of the women remaining on the show reacted too quickly and opened fire immediately, without assessing the situation, while five out of the nine or so remaining blokes passed. Once the shooting had stopped, the approaching soldier stood silently in front of the recruit and pointed to his badge.

Billy then increased the anxiety levels.

'*What the fuck are you doing?*' he shouted. 'He's one of ours! Why did you shoot him? Now you've got to explain to his wife and kids that he's dead.'

The mood was heavy. From the sidelines I noted every recruit's reactions as the truth was revealed to them, and for the women on the show the impact was visibly upsetting. Some of them even started to cry. It was a real eye-opener: I realized that in scary situations, such as the Marksmen Test, the female recruits on *SAS: Who Dares Wins* became more emotionally driven than the men and allowed their feelings to take charge, while over fifty per cent of the blokes on the show were happy to wait it out. They paused and thought: *Hang on, something's not right.* Most of the time they held off from pulling the trigger. (Though I wonder if the reaction would have been similar if a woman had been shouting the instructions rather than Billy. That would make for an interesting test.)

The emotion flooding through the female recruits was an understandable reaction, not only given the scientific findings by the University of Basel, but due to the way society has been shaped through history. A man being approached by a shouting stranger in a tunnel is likely to think: *What the fuck's going on here? This is a bit sketchy* . . . A woman will probably imagine the worst-case scenario: *I'm about to get attacked*. It's unsurprising that they might feel more vulnerable as a result.

Without exception, everybody – male and female – who endured the Marksmen Test was shocked by its emotional impact, probably because it delivered an insight into some of the more horrific realities of military operations. However, all of us have the potential to manage those unsettling emotions, with a little help from a technique I've called 'the Cigar Moment', which I illustrate in Phase Nine.

MEN AND WOMEN: WHO HIDES BEHIND WHO?

Without doubt, the levels of resilience and determination of the groups within *SAS: Who Dares Wins* diminish when the genders are mixed – the momentum drains away. That's not to say it's the fault of the female recruits or the males, but for some reason the mental grit of the collective seems to weaken. Some of the blokes become moody; they grumble and use the women around them as an excuse to put in less of a shift. Their response to sharing team tasks with members of the opposite sex often appears defeatist, the general attitude being: *How the fuck are we supposed to complete this task when we've got to work with physically weaker women?* Meanwhile, a number of women involved have happily lived up to a stereotypical position; they shy away from conflict and fail to impose themselves on tasks in a positive fashion. Their attitude appears to be: *We're physically weaker than these lads – what's the point of putting up a fight?* As a result, both groups become less productive.

One example of this took place during Series Five, when we arranged for a CASEVAC drill in which two male recruits had been incapacitated. Two mixed groups, Team Alpha and Team Bravo, were tasked with carrying them away. That meant that every woman still remaining on the show had to help with the heavy lifting alongside the men, but rather than involving themselves aggressively, nearly all the females apart from one (Carla Devlin, who we'll get on to later; interestingly she passed the Marksmen Test too) stood back and let the males take charge. Some of them started carrying their teammates' bergens, rather than helping with the lifting or navigation – one of them even fainted as a result. Meanwhile, the blokes involved didn't put in nearly as much legwork as they had in previous tests. In their heads, it was as if the women were giving them a ready-made excuse for failure, and their lack of positivity soon showed. From where I was standing they seemed sloppy and lazy.

The Directing Staff looked at one another in disbelief until, eventually, we decided to separate the sexes. Once everybody had been pooled into same-gender groups the work rate immediately improved. It was so weird. The women became stronger when lifting the injured recruits, as did the men's team, suggesting that each gender group had hidden behind the other. With their excuses stripped away, the females suddenly realized they couldn't hide behind the men and they imposed themselves on the test. Without a get-out-of-jail-free card to fall back on, the blokes stepped up to the plate with more aggression. Everybody improved as a result. The test became a race. The blokes finished first, but the women were only ninety seconds behind.

These reactions might partly be due to genetics. The SRY gene, which directs male development, is believed to cause aggression and the 'fight-or-flight' response. In 2012, researchers from Melbourne's Prince Henry's Institute of Medical Research wanted to discover why men tended to adopt a more aggressive position when experiencing negative emotions, and why women took a 'tend-and-befriend' route, which was more passive. The SRY gene found in men, they explained, was a sex-determining gene which 'secretes hormones that masculinise the developing body'. It's been discovered that SRY also lives in some of the major organs, such as the brain, lungs and heart. Dr Joohyung Lee, who helped conduct the study, argued that SRY affects a bloke's neural and cardio activity, which greatly influenced their response to stress. In other words, they either attacked or retreated.

Meanwhile, many women tend to be calmed down by the production of oestrogen and 'internal opiates', both of which help them to keep any aggressive reactions at a simmer. (Though given the results of the Marksmen Test, I could argue that this response differs according to the risk involved.) The theory is that they naturally adopt a tend-and-befriend approach – they *tend* to their young and *befriend* others – because increasing the size of their social group like this increases their odds of survival in times of danger – the idea being that a predator will be less likely to attack a group than it would an individual. Could it be that genes dissuaded the female recruits from showing aggression during the CASEVAC test? Certainly it might explain why the women hiding behind the men didn't challenge the decisions being made. Likewise, this scientific theory might also be the reason why the men behaved the way that they did – had the blokes hiding behind the women taken the 'flight' option in the fight-or-flight response?

So what can men and women working together do to overcome these issues? The answer, as with most problems, lies in communication and commitment. If an individual (male or female) is clearly weaker than the rest of the group in some areas, they should look to involve themselves in positive ways rather than hanging back, or overloading themselves with their teammates' equipment.

A good way to start would be to accept the differences as a group and use them as an advantage. In the case of the CASEVAC exercise, the weaker recruits should have offered to guide the stronger team members as they moved; during rest periods they could also have held the stretcher in situ for thirty seconds while the stronger individuals took a quick breather. Those resting would have been able to push themselves harder in the knowledge that there would be periodic breaks. Confident that they were working with equally dynamic partners, they would also have felt less scared of failure.

Too often in team events, individuals or small groups attempt to fit square pegs into round holes. They assign roles according to position and status rather than suitability. For example, the most senior member of a start-up company might be assigned the job of charming new investors at a conference, when it's the second-in-command who's actually the most engaging and articulate member of the group. In an elite military setting, however, everyone was put into operational teams according to their skill sets. The demolitions guy concentrated on his potentially lethal explosives; the radio operator concentrated on connecting all parties involved in the mission; the medic patched up the injured. There was no ego or rank, or disputes over who was best at what. Instead, the requirements for the mission were clinically assessed and a team of experts was put together according to suitability.

It takes courage for a non-military group to get to that point, though. It's hard for people to say, *I can't do this*. The answer is to respond with a positive suggestion. *But I can do that*. Be bold. Commit. A team can only move as quickly as their slowest members, so work to turn those individuals into assets.

THE SUBTLE ART OF IGNORING GENDER DISTRACTIONS

If men and women are to work together in a Special Forces capacity then the disruptive issues that can potentially divide them will have to be overcome. In other words, *they must shut out all the distractions*.

One female recruit to *SAS: Who Dares Wins* who managed this trick was Carla Devlin. A former Olympic rower and a mum of four, Carla arrived on the civilian version of the show in 2020 with something to prove: her profile had dropped a little since her appearance in Beijing 2008, and in 2018 she'd been diagnosed with breast cancer. Thankfully, she'd pulled through, but the worst-case scenario must have flashed through Carla's mind when doctors had initially diagnosed her condition because her mum had died from the same illness and, by the sound of it, Carla had endured a rough ride in the fallout – and she was tough. For whatever reason, gender didn't bother Carla and she wouldn't allow the blokes in her group to intimidate her. She certainly wasn't going to allow men to use her femininity as an excuse. She ignored the complicated relationships between the genders, borne out of genetics and centuries of real life, and thrived throughout the season.

From the off, I was inspired by Carla. She'd achieved so much in life. Rising up to a physical or emotional challenge was easy for her, so much so that at one point I thought she wasn't taking the show seriously. Mentally she seemed to find every situation a breeze, no doubt because she was used to being thrashed as part of her Olympic training. I'd even dragged her in for questioning because her attitude had annoyed me. We'd been forcing the recruits into a position of physical fatigue by working them in the freezing cold, but Carla had shrugged off the stress. She had a look that said, 'Oh yeah? You're going to order me to run up this hill again, are you? No problem . . .' Carla had realized it was all a game, like most soldiers do when they become a little longer in the tooth. And she didn't want to play in the same way as the others. Instead, she cracked on and shut out all the distractions: discomfort, the cold, fear, and men and women living and working together. None of it was a problem.

'You're too clever for this shit,' I said to her. 'You don't want to be doing this and I can see it.'

Carla became defensive. 'No, I really want to be here.'

'This is not me having a go at you. I'm giving you a compliment.'

I couldn't get my head around her being there. Carla had beaten cancer. She had four kids at home. *She was an Olympian.* Why would she give a shit about being on *SAS: Who Dares Wins?* At that point I'd wanted to bin her off, but I was wrong about her commitment. Against all expectations, Carla made it to the final four of Season Five. She was forty. A recruit has to be pretty special to make it through to the last day, and not too many people of that age can make the distance. At the very end, the test that broke her was another physical thrashing. We'd pushed the recruits through the capture-and-interrogation process, which was usually the last challenge of the show, but rather than ending the work there we'd decided to maintain the element of shock. Just when the final four started to believe their suffering was over, another challenge was thrown in – an event we referred to as a 'false ending'. The physical beastings started up again, and it was rough. In the end, the situation broke Carla and her armband, the identification number worn by every recruit, had to be taken away. She'd never have given it up on her own.

When the show was finished, a bottle of gin arrived for every member of the DS, accompanied by a handwritten note. It was from Carla, which further underlined how wrong I'd been about her attitude. *She was a better person than we were.* On mine it read: 'I know you thought I didn't want to be there, but I did. I wasn't too long in the tooth. I was finding out new things about myself.'

It served as an inspirational lesson. Carla Devlin possessed the right mentality; she carried exactly the type of personality for a unique set of circumstances and would have probably thrived in a mixed environment within the military elite. The key, as she had discovered, was to shut out all distractions, which is a skill we can all lean in to when becoming more resilient in a team environment.

But how can we do this?

The answer is to focus on the endgame: *What is it we're trying to achieve?* There's usually a lot of external noise going on during the challenges we might be involved in, sometimes literally. Professional footballers have to deal with the pressure of playing before huge crowds of screaming fans and a lot of them are yelling abuse. To fret about the personal insults would be to fail, because any distractions at that level can make the difference between winning and losing. Those who go on to be great players are often the ones with the ability to tune out the distractions around them.

It's a skill I've often relied upon. While filming Season Five of *SAS: Who Dares Wins*, the recruits were ordered to perform a drown-proofing test in a natural pool. One by one, we tied their hands together and ordered them to take a deep breath before dropping to the bottom, then springing back up as soon as their feet touched the bed. There were tonnes of distracting factors. The camera crew was moving around me and the conditions were grim: the water was brutally cold. I know because I remained in the pool for the duration of the test as a safety supervisor and my head ached every time I dipped under the water. It was as if somebody had slapped me around the skull, and when I looked up I noticed snow at the top of the nearby mountains. But I stayed switched on. I wasn't bothered by the presence of a camera crew; I knew that if I did my job and the crew did theirs, everything would go according to plan. Instead, I focused on the safety of the recruits, ensuring the test was conducted exactly as it should have been. The distractions soon faded away.

This same attitude has to be implemented in men and women when operating together in military situations. Any discomfort is an irrelevance; all efforts should be focused on the mission and how best to execute the established plan. If a woman is to make it into the military elite, it will only happen if everyone working around her can overcome the subtle and not-so-subtle differences between genders. The reality is this: in war there's no time for niceties; there's very little room for being squeamish or feeling uncomfortable in front of members of the opposite sex. Everybody has to be treated the same, regardless of gender. The only people that can operate in a hostile environment successfully are the Right People. And if that means a mixture of men and women working effectively and powerfully at the sharp end of military life, getting the job done, then who cares about the gender of the individuals in the group?

OPERATIONAL DEBRIEF

▶▶ Gender is irrelevant when it comes to resilience. I know women who are as tough as nails and blokes who shrink at the first sign of a battle. Generally, there are two types of people when it comes to resilience: those that have it and those that haven't yet found it.

▶▶ From my experience of watching male and female recruits working together on *SAS: Who Dares Wins*, men and women show resilience in different ways. As the Marksmen Test proved, women can be a bit more emotionally driven under extreme psychological pressure (though one male recruit, Chris, a very emotional individual, actually ran into the tunnel while firing his weapon, causing Billy to call him a 'bellend'). But they're also more considered and tactical when planning a task – they tend-and-befriend. Blokes can be more headstrong when faced with a mission. Due to their fight-or-flight response, they sometimes rush into their own deaths, but, in the main, they tend to remain calmer when responding to anger or other negative emotions. (As Chris proved, there will always be exceptions.)

▶▶ If men and women are to mix within an elite military operation, all individuals will need to be of a similar mindset. Teamwork, honesty and communication are key. Egos and gender stereotypes have to be left at the door. There's no room for niceties or awkwardness when working in extremes. If those psychological roadblocks can be negotiated, as Carla Devlin proved, then there may be a way that men and women can work together in the most specialized units within the British military.

SITUATIONAL AWARENESS

OPERATIONAL ARGUMENTS BETWEEN MEN AND WOMEN – AND HOW TO SOLVE THEM

As detailed in Phase Four, personal disputes aren't allowed to affect us in the Special Forces Brotherhood. As a group of operators, it's imperative we function effectively and with unity. Issues with others or ego clashes never come into play during a gunfight – they can't. To still be fuming over a missed round of teas or a squabble in the mess simply won't work when missions begin. Meanwhile, sulking over a decision that hasn't gone in our favour only distracts us from the job in hand.

If ever I had a problem with another individual during a military tour, I always compartmentalized the disagreement and worked with the lads as if nothing had happened. It was the only way to complete the required work without injury or fatalities. This attitude towards disputes has also applied to other team environments where cohesion is key. The former Manchester United footballers Teddy Sheringham and Andy Cole couldn't stand one another yet they made up one of the most effective strike forces in Premiership football during the late 1990s. Alliance regardless of personal dispute is always possible – but it's bloody difficult.

In order to create unity and shared purpose, one trick used before elite operations was to emphasize the mission aim during every brief. To do so, the overall objective was repeated twice. Once a plan had been detailed, the Ground Commander would remind the group: 'Our mission today is to rescue Hostage X.' The detail was then repeated so every operator was clear as to why they were going into such a hostile environment, followed again by: 'Our job today is to rescue Hostage X.' I've since found that it's important to apply this mental process to all jobs of significance – a clear sense of objective is important for the success of any mission, even the ones we wish we didn't have to conduct in the first place, with people we really can't stand.

For example, an experienced male scientist might be forced into a group project with an equally experienced female colleague. In the past, the pair of them had disagreed over each other's findings and so the potential for conflict is high. However, if their cause is important – the research of a life-saving vaccine or the development of a groundbreaking cancer treatment – it's usually enough for them to keep their minds on the job. Repeating their overall objective in these situations is imperative to remain on course. In this case: 'We're working together to save lives . . . *We're working together to save lives.*'

All it takes is a little focus and a reminder of what we're hoping to achieve together – our primary mission.

We're going to pass that exam together.
We're going to finish writing that script together.
We're going to break that personal best together.
Focus on the objective. Say it out loud. Then repeat.

PHASE SIX

THE POWER OF HONESTY:
HANDLING THE TRUTH

Honesty is a vital asset when building resilience because it teaches us the power of brutal assessment, where acceptance of a negative situation brings tactical strength. Sadly, a lot of people would rather lie to themselves about their reality, especially when they're in the shit. They claim to enjoy their job when the daily workload is causing them to crack. They convince themselves that a partner's behaviour is OK when actually it's laced with toxicity. They pretend to have a handle on the vices causing them emotional and physical damage. But if they acted truthfully about their issues and weaknesses, they'd quickly make the first steps towards overcoming them.

Honesty and integrity are also valuable assets in intelligence-gathering scenarios. In a military sense, assessing information based solely on the facts, without opinion or judgement, is regarded as the only way to paint an accurate picture of a situation, such as a terrorist training camp or a narcotics-trafficking cell. In surveillance ops, honesty and integrity allow a specialist soldier to look at the information available to them and make a judgement call. They can then build a more robust battle plan and their attack becomes more resilient as a result. In a civilian setting, if people were to base their most important decisions on hard facts, rather than beliefs and emotions, they'd be less surprised by any unpleasant results.

But being honest with ourselves is often the toughest call to make. (How many of us respond accurately when the doctor quizzes us about our alcohol intake, or truly push ourselves as hard as we can in that gym class?) But if we can stomach it, answering painful, personal questions in a truthful way is often the fast track to a more resilient profile. Honesty helps us to grow. And in growth we can become so much tougher.

HONESTY ABOUT FAILURE

No plan survives contact. It's a basic fact of war. (Or, as Mike Tyson once famously said, 'Everyone has a plan until they get punched in the face.') As you can imagine, I've lived Tyson's theory for real, sometimes on a daily basis, and rarely did a military operation go to plan, 100 per cent, from beginning to end. This can also be said of the many projects or challenges we undertake in normal life: the new job, a physical effort, the rehabilitation from injury or accident, a house move, a wedding . . . The list goes on and on. During each example, unexpected hitches and fuck-ups can upend the best-laid plans, no matter how much preparation has taken place in advance. The key to overcoming a Mike Tyson-style smack to the gob is to first accept its likelihood of happening. The next step is to react accordingly when it does.

At this point, let me give you a typically extreme case study. During one military tour, we were on the hunt for a nasty militia leader. Our intel had revealed his position in a small town at the foot of a mountain range, an area we knew to be fairly sketchy. (The biggest hint that somebody of importance had been hidden there was the fact that somebody usually opened fire on us whenever we flew nearby.) Having settled on a date of attack, we went in at night, flying across a series of hills in choppers before landing on a flat stretch of desert safely short of our target. The plan was to then walk across deadly ground, reaching the town at sun-up, and kick in a few doors, at which point our person of interest would hopefully surface.

We moved along the terrain as a long line of men, in an attempt to go undetected by any enemy fighters along the way. The sky was pitch black. Everyone tried their best to stay quiet and the only noise was the crunch of our boots on the rock and sand. Every now and then the eerie chatter of gunfire opened up in the distance. *Bup-bup-bup-bup. Bup-bup-bup-bup.* A scrap had kicked off several miles away and through the grainy-green of my night-vision goggles I watched flashes of light – either explosions or mortar blasts – bursting across the horizon.

Probably the Yanks getting into some trouble, I thought, pressing ahead.

Even though I was in the middle of a war zone, where rockets and tracer fire were lighting up the sky, I felt wrapped up in a cocoon. It felt peaceful, like I was a million miles away from the madness elsewhere, and I was reminded of once being on a passenger flight on Bonfire Night. Inside the plane there had been nothing but the soothing, muffled roar of air conditioning and engines. But outside, hundreds of fireworks were flickering and exploding across the blackness in a weird blend of calm and chaos. The vibe in the desert was just as eerily serene.

Then a dog barked in the distance. And another. I hated the mutts in those countries. I never knew what breed they were, but they were big, mean and crazy. Their eyes were usually bloodshot because of the dust and crap in the air, which gave them a rabid appearance. The locals liked to cut their ears off to make them look even more intimidating. Whenever one approached me – snarling and growling – I'd try to frighten it off with a boot. I didn't fancy losing a chunk from my arm or leg. And while I'd been jabbed for rabies and plenty of other debilitating infections, I didn't fancy putting those vaccinations to the test.

The barking was the dogs' worst trait, though. They rarely stayed quiet, even in the dead of night, and the local animals had obviously caught our scent. *Now they wanted to tell everybody about it.* We still had some distance to cover – I could just about make out the edges of the buildings through my goggles – but our smell must have carried on the wind. Suddenly, heavy gunfire echoed behind us. It was much louder and much closer than the shooting we'd heard earlier. I recognized the sound of a DShK, or 'Dushka', the Soviet heavy machine gun. Their rounds seemed to land behind us, exploding in the footprints we'd made five minutes ago.

'Is that for us?' I said, looking around as more gunfire zipped overhead.

Nobody seemed to know for certain, though an awful realization seemed to settle into the group: *it was too close to have been a coincidence.* 'Well, they're firing at something. Let's crack on a bit . . .'

We advanced for another ten minutes. Every now and then, rounds from the Dushka ripped open the sky above us and *ka-boom*ed into the rock and sand at our rear. Our paranoia had risen. *They must know we're out here – just not where, exactly.* A pilot circling above confirmed our worst fears moments later:

'Lads, there are shitloads of personal security on the ground,' crackled a voice in our comms. 'They're positioned all around the town. Keep on your toes.'

I peered into the black. I couldn't see anything or anyone, but I got the feeling we were walking into a trap. We would later find out that spotters had been positioned in the mountains and were directing several defensive outposts around the town. Snipers were lying in wait. Once we got close enough, the order to open fire would have been given. An ambush was going to be bad enough but that wasn't the worst of it. Somebody suddenly raised a hand: we had to stop moving.

'*Wait* . . . They're setting up ambushes. There are several ten-man teams waiting for us in ditches . . .'

Fucking hell.

We'd suspected that we were in for a heavy scrap that night. The bloke we were after was a big name on the Allied Forces' Most Wanted list; he was a nasty character with some serious influence among the enemy militia we were engaged with. It made sense that he would be fairly well guarded; we just hadn't expected him to be *this* well guarded. There was a pause as we figured out our next steps: *should we push on or turn back?* Then an unnerving comment came out of the dark.

'Er, hang on a minute.' It was Mooro, a mate of mine. 'What the fuck have we walked into?' He was pointing to several black spots on the ground around him.

I peered down at the sand. In the dark it was almost impossible at first to discern any distinct shapes, but as I scanned the space around me I noticed the black circular disc of an anti-personnel landmine. Then another. And another. Dozens of them had been scattered across the ground and we were surrounded by them. It was a miracle nobody had trodden on one. Anyone making the wrong step would have been blown to pieces.

'Whoa! Don't step on the black things!' shouted another voice.

'We'll have to chin this off,' said somebody behind me. 'We're not going to surprise them now, and nothing's in our favour. Let's walk back to the landing zone, call in a heli and head back to base . . .'

There were a few groans of disappointment. I felt annoyed too. It was probably one of the very few times where we'd had to chuck in the towel on an operation at such an early stage, but we really had no other option. We were screwed; the odds of success were too slim and there was no point pretending otherwise. By honestly accepting that we were in a bad situation, we were allowing ourselves the opportunity to fight another day. Had we ignored the truths around us and made an aggressive judgement call, we might have suffered some serious casualties. Plus, our enemy would have landed a morale-boosting victory. It was far better to make a considered assessment of a sketchy situation and to retreat. *We'd underestimated the strength of our enemy. We were outnumbered. Taking a backwards step was the smartest thing to do.*

The decision was borne from experience. We'd long been trained that in order to act as a resilient force, it was tactically astute to be brutally honest about a failing plan, but only if we learned from our losses. In that respect, the mission had been fairly successful. Sure, we hadn't grabbed the bloke we'd been looking for, but we were 100 per cent positive that our person of interest, or somebody just as important, was hiding away in that town. Why would there have been so much security if a nobody was living there? In that respect, the operation was a score. A week or so later, we heard that our target had been taken down by an aerial attack. No British troops were injured in the process. *The honesty about our failure had turned defeat into victory.*

If only people thought along the same logical lines outside of service. How many times do we hear of individuals following up on bad ideas, even as the potential for failure becomes increasingly obvious? We stay with jobs that make us increasingly unhappy. We ignore the alarm bells ringing on our physical health, relationships, finances or emotional well-being because we think that to re-evaluate them would be to admit defeat. We chuck away good money to salvage bad ideas. Rather than thinking tactically and reassessing a situation at regular intervals, we pretend everything is OK. *We lie to ourselves.* We fall victim to our own egos, convinced that to take a step back from a situation will represent a disaster or embarrassment. But it's important to know that, in a shitshow, retreating is sometimes the most positive step a person or team can make.

HONESTY ABOUT SELF

Honesty is arguably the most difficult asset to utilize when building resilience because it requires us to ask some rough questions of ourselves – and then answer with some ugly home truths. For example, following on from a failed relationship, it's sometimes vital we take a long look at our character flaws or our behaviour. It might be that some of the negative traits in our personalities require a little work, especially if we're to avoid making the same mistakes again. Whatever our screw-ups, it never hurts to take a look in the mirror and ask the question: *How did I fuck that up? And how can I un-fuck the problem?* But the process can be challenging and destabilizing, as I found out during the aftershocks of my departure from the military.

My life was in tatters. I felt shame at the way in which I left a job I'd loved. I mourned a career that had once defined me as a person and a man. I was caught up in a series of toxic relationships that had destabilized my emotional well-being and I'd cut away the Brotherhood that had played such a valuable part in keeping me positive during stressful times. I found myself in a new job that I hated, where I worked in a role as far removed from my life behind enemy lines as I could imagine. However, instead of accepting my position and looking for ways to improve it, I pretended everything was OK. I bullshitted myself. The cover-up very nearly killed me.

I became so depressed that I contemplated suicide. Luckily, I had second thoughts and there was enough resilience in the tank to keep me going. From there I had to admit some painful facts about where my life was headed. Bloody hell, the process still plays on my mind because it was so painful, but if I'd avoided the tough questions I wouldn't be around today. In a brutally honest assessment, I looked at all the situations that were affecting me negatively and worked to turn them into positives.

Having accepted I was on the verge of suicide, I worked with friends to find a therapist who was suited to my personality and issues. Luckily, I was able to locate one pretty quickly. I cut away some of the toxic relationships that were taking place in my life, because they were dragging me in the wrong direction. It might have appeared to some of the people involved that I was being selfish or extreme, but I needed to change my situation for the better. (And throwing myself into the sea would have been a far more selfish act than breaking away from certain friends and partners.) Figuring out which parts of my old job I'd enjoyed, I decided I wanted to work outdoors; I needed to challenge myself physically while helping others, as I had done in service. With my *SAS: Who Dares Wins* mate Ollie Ollerton, I set up an elite military-style training programme for civilians called Break-Point. I then started the Rock2Recovery project mentioned earlier. By doing so, I bonded with a new brotherhood; thanks to therapy and a process of social rebuilding, I was then able to reconnect with my old circle of friends, without shame or embarrassment.

Sounds easy on paper, doesn't it? Well, it wasn't. But with time, like the phases on Selection, my honest self-assessment, while difficult, became doable. The hardest part was the first step: *I was truthful about myself.* It's a very human response not to want to endure pain, but like my life in the military, I needed to become comfortable within an uncomfortable situation. I admitted that my life was in a shit state and that a lot of my problems were self-made because I'd allowed myself to fall into a negative mindset. Yes, I'd been suffering from PTSD, which was a natural reaction to living an extreme life with the armed forces, but I'd believed, wrongly, that there was a stigma attached to my condition. And so I covered up my problems rather than talking to my old friends from the military, lads who would have expressed empathy for my pain. (I know this because when I reunited with them again at a party a year or so later, they were understanding and accepting.) Therapy helped me to come to terms with all of that.

I was then honest about my purpose. Once I'd been lucky enough to get a job on *SAS: Who Dares Wins*, I decided to use the platform as an exercise in honesty. I opened up about my mental health issues on TV and in media interviews, hoping it would help others to recognize any problems they might have too. I also detailed my struggles in *Battle Scars*. I've since been approached by men and women from all walks of life who have explained how the writing encouraged them to ask some painfully honest questions of their own. A number of them were military; others had been affected by a different type of trauma. Being able to help those people in some way gave me a sense of purpose.

Of course, there were regrets about some of my behaviour; I wasn't particularly proud of certain things I'd done in life. I'm human. All of us have made mistakes and nobody's perfect. But by being honest I was able to at least right some of the wrongs I'd committed and eventually my day-to-day life became easier. The changes didn't take place overnight, though, and there was always plenty of hard work ahead – there still is – but gradually, more and more positivity arrived in my life.

Honesty had become a part of the recovery process.

Following the first season of *SAS: Who Dares Wins*, after I'd admitted my breakdown to a large TV audience, I was asked whether I was worried about the public perception of me.

I thought, *Why the fuck have I got to worry about how people see me now? I've laid it all out there. I don't need to stress about putting up a make-believe bravado to feed my ego. My cards are on the table. I've said: 'This is me.' I've nothing to hide any more.*

The emotions and circumstances that had led me to rock bottom weren't unique. (In Phase Eleven we'll look more closely at how to spot the warning signs, because it can be difficult to recognize trouble when you're in the thick of a meltdown.) And not everybody needs to reach their lowest point to benefit from this process. Some people keep missing their work or personal targets without ever realizing why, but brutal self-honesty is a great way of shining a light on our weak spots.

None of us are bulletproof, either; all of us can be broken by life, often when we least expect it. Sometimes it only takes one shove. I've heard of people whose successful businesses were ruined by a negative relationship with alcohol. They lost their driving licence following a drunken offence. Unable to use the car, their livelihood went down the pan. In the wake of financial collapse, their home, family and prospects disintegrated until they were left with only the bare bones of a life. In other cases, perfectly natural events have sent people into a spin. Recently, a psychology student got in touch, having heard about my struggle with mental health problems. She wanted to use my story as a case study. During a phone call the student then explained how she'd followed a similar path to mine, having suffered from post-natal depression. Apparently she'd had a grim time of it. Just as a gunfight too many had triggered my step towards the edge, so childbirth had broken her.

Regardless of the cause, it takes a resilient mind to handle emotional turbulence successfully, but there are many ways to cope. During a life-altering experience, such as the diagnosis of a chronic illness, if a person has been brutally honest about the changes to come, there's a good chance they'll be able to manage the process more effectively. They may even have put one or two coping mechanisms in place to help themselves, such as a regular social event or a support network they can call upon. Denial during these periods can occasionally prove problematic, mainly because the shock of such a huge lifestyle shift is pretty overwhelming. I soon realized that my mindset in the fallout of leaving the military hadn't been too dissimilar to what many other people go through when they lose their job, or when they break up with a partner. I'd been deluding myself.

My new life was a jolt.

I certainly wasn't honest prior to being medically discharged with PTSD. It was set to be a life-changing moment and I ignored the truths about my new reality. I didn't ready myself; I lived the lie that I'd be experiencing a new beginning where everything was going to be cool once I'd woken up on my first day outside of the military. I hadn't considered the drastic changes to my identity and day-to-day routines because I was scared to acknowledge them. It was hard for me to imagine that

I'd become completely lost. The inevitable shift, when it arrived, was difficult to cope with at first.

What I needed was to be honest, and it was a lesson I've since learned the hard way. These days, if ever I'm asked for advice, or whenever a new intake at Rock2Recovery has asked me for help, I often use the same line: *honesty is everything.*

'The best way for you to look at this situation now, as hard as it is, is to see that you're on a positive journey,' I've explained. 'At some point, you're going to find a new you. But – and there is a but – you'll have to be honest with yourself first.'

There are people who will always play the victim. They want everything to be fixed for them, rather than by them, and that's fine. But they'll never really get to the bottom of what's breaking them down or weakening their chances of success, because without honesty they'll remain blind. The first step towards really resolving whatever issues have taken a person to breaking point – such as underlying feelings of rejection, failure, grief, anger, fear or resentment – or have caused them to miss their targets, is to self-assess during a period of brutal truth. It's not easy. In fact, it can be bloody horrible. I know, because being truthful with myself was such an excruciating moment. But once it was done I was able to piece my life together and grow. I'd understood exactly what I needed to do.

While this might sound like a tricky process at first, one effective way to kick-start an episode of long-term change is to answer some pretty difficult questions – with unflinching honesty. What those questions might be is completely down to you. However, the clue to their validity lies in the process. If they're uncomfortable, then they're probably on point. They might include the following:

- Am I happy – *really*?
- What's my purpose?
- Does my partner bring out the best in me?
- Where or when am I most fulfilled?
- If there were no financial pressures, expectations or rules, what would I do with my life?
- Fear or purpose: what drives me on?

Don't mess about. Get a pad and paper, then figure out your own questions and answer them ruthlessly. The process will give you clarity. It will also shove you in the right direction towards rethinking your position, whatever that might be. A greater understanding of the situation will follow afterwards.

HONESTY ABOUT INTEL

Facts get manipulated. The truth becomes distorted; sometimes accidentally, sometimes with intent. You only have to look at some of the people operating in British politics, or in the media, to understand this sad reality, though even when people have used statistics to spin inaccurate headlines or, in some cases, to tell outright lies, they're usually found out in the end. (Whether anything is done about the people responsible for the spinning during the fallout is often debatable.)

However, when it came to analysing facts during operations

for the British military, there was very little room for spin, opinion or interpretation. In order to be successful – and therefore resilient – an operator had to be brutally honest.

Nowhere was this attitude more important than when we were engaged on a surveillance operation. The specialist units of the British military were often called upon to watch enemy targets for information. We might have had eyes on a terrorist cell operating from an urban address, on drug traffickers in the desert, or on a militia training camp in a mountain hideaway. At times, life on a surveillance operation was pretty grim. We might have to literally dig a hole in the ground a few miles away from our target, or cut our way into foliage, to get a suitable, undetectable position from which to observe the comings and goings of whomever we were tailing. There were times where I had to stay in one place for a couple of weeks, living off dried food. While we were taking notes of what we'd been watching through our optics equipment, I found it important to remember one of the mantras of the military elite: *integrity is all you've got*.

Humans have a tendency to be swayed by popular opinion, or to let misinterpretation creep into fact. But in my line of work I was taught that unbiased honesty was imperative. On observation jobs it was my duty to report only what I saw and heard, and to draw any conclusions from that limited information was pointless and dangerous. It served as nothing more than speculation. For example, I might have been watching a building known to be a long-term hideout for some unpleasant individuals. During the operation, it would have been my role to log when they entered the building and when they left. The car they drove and the locations they parked in were reported too. Any opinions on what they might have been doing in there were irrelevant because those ideas were not backed up by fact. I could have guessed that they were planning a terrorist attack from that position, or building a bomb, but what hard evidence did I have? (Unless of course I saw them wearing hazmat suits while carefully handling a box bulging with wires. Then it would have been a different story altogether.) I had to stick to the facts and nothing else.

Why? Well, to be swayed by external ideas and to express them would have been misleading, and to mislead was highly dangerous when the stakes were so high, as they often were in a surveillance operation. It might be that, unbeknown to us, the people of interest operating out of that building had moved on and a new group, entirely innocent of any wrongdoing, had come in. Raiding them would result in a massive waste of time and money, and would freak out the people inside. It was vital that, in a line of work such as ours, the facts were dealt with honestly, impartially and without opinion, because intel was everything. That's also the case if it's the information we carry about ourselves, such as the honest answers to those all-too-painful questions about our weaknesses I mentioned earlier.

Of course, not every situation is cut and dried; two people in the same position might see things very differently. When writing *Battle Scars*, I described a moment where fear had temporarily freaked me out. I'd stepped off a helicopter during a mission where we had been massively outnumbered by an unexpectedly large and aggressive hostile force. It was a night raid, and chaos kicked off in the darkness. Bullets and mortar blasts tore through the air around me; one of our lads was killed almost the moment we'd touched down. Having briefly taken cover in a ditch, we worked our way through the trees towards an enemy compound.

I'd been tasked with leading the entry team. But as we got closer, two enemy fighters opened fire with AK-47s. With my night-vision goggles on, I wasn't sure whether they were taking desperate potshots, just hoping to hit something, or if they could actually see us – their aim seemed a little off. We took our time, crawling closer before dropping them in a burst of fire. At the noise, another fighter staggered from a doorway. He was carrying a wounded mate on his shoulder. A couple of rounds rocked him to the floor, too, but as he fell, I spotted a boy standing behind him. He can't have been more than five years old. Dressed in a football shirt that was several sizes too big and carrying a teddy bear, he was screaming. I wanted to get him to safety, but before I had a chance to reach out, he ran into the trees. Somebody shouted out on the comms: *Slow down a bit! There are civilians in the area.* Later, when I went through therapy, I spoke of how that lad in his football kit had haunted me as I drove around Hampshire and Surrey for my civilian job during 2012, my mental health on the brink.

When *Battle Scars* was published, one of the lads who had been alongside me during the mission called me up to say he'd read it. 'But I'm a bit confused,' he said. 'That kid you saw on the operation . . . *There was no kid.*'

'What are you talking about? I saw him.'

'Yeah, but I didn't, mate, and I was standing right next to you.'

I couldn't work it out. I'd seen him as clear as day, and the fact that doubt was being cast on my recollection put me into a bit of a spin. I started to wonder about myself in all the stress and terror, and I questioned whether the boy had actually been there at all. The senses tend to become overloaded in a gun battle of that kind; the mind tries to pick out which noises to worry about and which ones to ignore, and that can be pretty troublesome in the middle of a scrap. Working with night-vision goggles on can be a little disorientating too. They say the brain takes in hundreds of thousands of different bits of information every second. That process must run at a greater speed during combat situations where there are people running around, explosions going off and enemy fighters trying to kill you. Then again, my mate might have been looking the other way for a split second, during which the boy had appeared (and hadn't put two and two together about the new intel regarding civilians in the area). Or maybe his mind had been protecting itself, shutting out the memory because it was too distressing to acknowledge.

So, thinking about it, it's really no surprise that one of us might have got it wrong. The important thing was that I saw what *I thought* was factually correct in the moment and I later wrote about it honestly. In a flashpoint situation of that kind, had we not heard the shout over our comms, it would have been my job to tell the people around me exactly what I had seen. If I'd stopped to think, *Is he really there?* or, *Where did he come from?* and second-guessed myself in the moment, I might have behaved differently from that point on. Instead, we slowed things down and reassessed our situation. The aggression in our work changed ever so slightly from that moment on, and our new approach was a little more cautious. I like to think it prevented an unpleasant accident from happening.

If my recollection was wrong, I'll put my hand up to it. Fine. *So be it.* It's not as if anybody failed on the mission because of my experience. If anything, with both my mate and me being truthful about our understanding of the situation afterwards, we probably learned a lesson about perspective. *But at least we'd been honest.* In the big, wide world, people try to cover up their mistakes or uncertainties. They promise one thing and then pretend to have said another when things don't work out the way they'd have liked. They screw up and keep quiet, hoping that nobody will notice – or, worse, they blame it on somebody else. I experienced that situation all too often when I started working in the service industry and it drove me crackers.

As a specialist operator I was trained to 'fess up to any mistake, no matter how small, because the implications for not mentioning it might have been disastrous. If I lost a valuable piece of equipment or forgot to mention a scrap of intel during an operational debrief, I never kept quiet about it in the hope that my error would go unnoticed. Instead, I raised my hand afterwards, I apologized for the mistake and then figured out how best to un-fuck the situation I'd created. Any intel I added was then assessed and factored into the work we'd been conducting at the time. Equipment I might have left behind was replaced and made available for use, with nobody left exposed by its absence. Honesty kept my unit strong and our practices intact, whereas not being straight about my failings would have led to a nasty surprise further down the line, one that might have left us weakened in a dangerous situation.

The realilty is that an individual can grow and become more effective by being honest at all times, both with themselves and with others. When it comes to assessing a situation, work only with the available facts, because everything beyond that is pure speculation. If those facts put us in a bad light, so be it. Covering them up will only expose us later on. Sticking to the truth is the best route to building a resilient character.

OPERATIONAL DEBRIEF

》 Honesty and integrity are everything in the military elite. Brutal self-assessment allows us to function more effectively as operators and to grow as individuals.

》 When self-assessing, ask the questions that make you most uncomfortable: *Am I happy? Am I fulfilled? What life would give me purpose? Do the people in my life bring out the best in me?* Honest answers to tough questions of this kind can help us to become stronger.

》 Intel is valuable when working towards resilience, but only if it's dealt with honestly. Try to make assessments using fact rather than opinion. Basing a judgement or decision solely on speculation and guesswork can lead to trouble.

》 Honesty and integrity is everything when working towards resilience. If you fuck up, 'fess up. If you don't know the answer to something, say so rather than bluffing. Forgotten to complete a task? Don't blame it on someone else; show integrity and admit it. Nobody likes nasty surprises, no matter what their situation. Operating truthfully helps to avoid them.

SITUATIONAL AWARENESS

FAILURE AS A LESSON

Failure. I hate that word. It's the finality of it that bothers me: the idea that once a person has screwed up, they're judged negatively or binned off. The reality of failure is very different, however. To not succeed immediately, or to mess something up, is actually a moment to be savoured. *It's an opportunity to pause and learn.* In fact, failure is only the end if we allow it to dominate our thinking. If we can reframe mistakes as an educational experience, their negative impacts are usually diminished more quickly, whereas dwelling on them with regret or shame only prolongs the pain.

In a military sense, I blundered very early on in my career while working through Basic Training with the Royal Marines as a naive sixteen-year-old. We were on a 'Criteria Exercise', a tactical drill that was supposed to teach us about standing patrols where a unit or soldier had to sit and watch a particular area, such as an enemy supply route or a potentially hostile rendezvous point. During the training session my unit was bumped by a mock enemy attack. We were ordered to retreat and in the chaos I left my day sack behind. The blunder was set to land me in some serious hot water. The training team were going to beast me once the exercise was concluded and I knew it. That one mistake played on my mind all day.

When the rollicking arrived, it was full-on. My screw-up had serious consequences and I was harshed. After the shouting had stopped, the training team informed me I was being held back. That meant I'd have to leave my mates behind and join another troop so I could retake the exercise in a couple of weeks. I was then warned that if I failed the exercise again I'd be kicked out of Basic Training. The experience was demoralizing. I became furious with myself. The implications of my actions caused me to go into a bit of a downward spiral because I knew the lads I'd been training with for months were going to pass out ahead of me and I wouldn't get to share in that celebratory moment with them. I was gutted.

Once I'd got over the initial disappointment, I decided to turn my negative into a positive. I was honest about my mistake; I didn't blame others, or the situation. Instead, I got on with the work in hand because a valuable learning opportunity had been presented to me. I'd been so scarred by leaving my day sack behind that I became desperate to improve. I took meticulous care of my kit, weapon and personal belongings and I was soon a better soldier as a result. It was clear to me that being a Royal Marine was a serious business and attention to detail was vital. It was as if I could suddenly grasp what was expected of me at all times, which had probably been the intention of the training team when they'd dished out their punishment. That attitude lasted throughout my military career and left a permanent mark on me.

Sometimes we can suffer due to an event entirely beyond our control. Redundancies happen, leaving us unemployed. Loved ones unexpectedly pass away and our daily lives change beyond recognition. Political decisions alter our day-to-day existence, sometimes in horrible ways. In those moments we have to find the positive strand that can help us to move on. As with the mistakes we make in our lives, freak occurrences, too, deliver an educational opportunity. Redundancies can open us up to different career possibilities. The death of a relative shows us new ways to care for the people around us. An unpleasant political decision might encourage us to work for change, by joining a group or volunteering for a cause.

Taking lessons from failure or bad situations was a good way of operating successfully in war, too. As I've mentioned, negativity was contagious in flashpoints. People with a moody, glass-half-empty attitude rarely made it into the military elite, if ever, because pessimism or a fearful attitude in sketchy moments led to failed missions and maximum casualties. But to accept mistakes and unexpected misfortune as learning experiences was the most effective route out of trouble. It was yet another mark of the Thinking Soldier.

PHASE SEVEN

SELF-AWARENESS:
DEFEAT YOUR DEMONS

Self-awareness is everything when striving for resilience. How can we negotiate our weaknesses if we're unsure of what they might be in the first place? And if we're to reach our maximum potential, we need to be aware of our strengths, too. When a ruthlessly self-aware individual strives for success, they'll have a fair idea of the emotional pitfalls to watch out for and the personal assets in their armoury – or, in other words, the tools needed to circumnavigate their vulnerabilities.

That's the good news. The bad news is that most of us haven't conducted a 360-degree personal evaluation because being honest about our flaws is scary. That's not to say it can't be figured out, and a little graft and analysis can give everyone a deeper understanding of what makes them tick, as we discussed in Phase Six.

Self-awareness is incredibly important because it enables us to identify and tackle some of the emotional issues that can derail us as we work towards our goals. By understanding the personal demons

that can challenge us, and learning how to defeat them, we're able to
build a greater level of resilience . . .

EMOTIONAL SELF-AWARENESS
AND NEGATIVE THOUGHT

We all have our strengths, but all of us have the Demon too –
that hang-up, phobia or psychological roadblock that causes us
to fail, make bad decisions or behave in a way that's debilitating
to ourselves and to others. The Demon might arrive as a doubting voice in the head or a surge of fear. Sometimes it takes the
form of emotional paralysis and can shut us down during
moments of high stress; it prevents us from functioning effectively or pushes us into losing our temper. But these negative
forces are part of us – wounds from some past trauma, or an
unresolved issue that nags away at our thinking, sometimes
consciously, other times subconsciously. If we can understand
those demons, if we can get a grasp on our true nature through
self-awareness, then we can become incredibly resilient to any
obstacles standing in our path.

Just as some soldiers are able to fight through extreme pain in
do-or-die events, so we all have the potential to push past the
negative thoughts dragging us back. Imagine someone with an
unhealthy lifestyle. They might feel unwilling to get off their
arse if they've had an uncomfortable or embarrassing gym
experience in the past. Stepping into the weights room might fill
them with an intense dread. However, this is a state of mind and
a situation that's easily rectifiable through positive action. A

little self-awareness regarding motivation and energy levels is important, too. To overcome their hang-ups, that particular person should think: *The past is gone and I need to get a little fitter. It makes sense to attack the treadmill when I'm feeling emotionally strongest. I'm most proactive in the mornings. Let's attack the day early on . . .*

These stresses are relative. The fearful gym-goer can feel just as scared as the person with a terror of heights, flying or enclosed spaces. I know about this emotional friction because negative feelings were a potential challenge for me during war, as they were for everybody I fought alongside. If it wasn't handled correctly, fear could cause an operator to second-guess their actions; they might hesitate in a moment where speed was required. Anger was a dangerous reaction to an attack or a violent situation, and had to be suppressed. (In gun battles, hot-headedness was the worst kind of response, and people who flared up or acted without thinking were usually the first to get dropped.) Elsewhere, sadness or grief for a lost teammate might cause a person to lose focus. All of those emotions were occupational hazards in war because life was scary, situations were brutal, and friends died. The only way to operate in those scenarios was to use self-awareness as a way of controlling the controllable.

But how?

In my case, I handled those feelings first by accepting them as they emerged and acknowledging their presence. I then managed them rationally: if I was scared, I accepted the fear. I told myself I was frightened because an incredibly dangerous situation was kicking off. I then used the emotion to concentrate. If

I became angry, I generally calmed myself with the knowledge that rational thought was imperative when working successfully in dangerous operations. Grief was compartmentalized and managed when I had time for reflection. With these processes, I became more emotionally resilient. That might sound unbelievably cold, but really there was no other option.

Broken down, this process can be easily recalled as the three rules of basic psychological admin:

1) Accept: Give any negative emotions the respect they deserve and acknowledge them.
2) Understand: Remember you're human. Sadly, feeling shit or fucking up is part of the experience sometimes.
3) Resolve: Work out how to fix the problem and move ahead.

Let's take grief as a case study. I've been in more situations than I'd care to remember where people I knew, or cared for, were killed or seriously hurt, but with self-awareness I was able to manage my feelings and reactions.

In the immediate aftermath of a mission where someone had been killed, as the lads squared away their kit in the equipment cage, it was easy to feel upended for a few moments. But there was no time to grieve or freak out. All of us had a job to do and the post-mission debrief went ahead as usual. Nobody would pretend that it hadn't happened, and the death was always acknowledged by the group and the Officer Commanding; there would be a moment to reflect, and then we were expected to crack on with the next job.

The impact was just as heavy when an operator had been seriously injured. I remember seeing a teammate being dragged away by the medic during a Door-Kicking raid. He'd taken at least one round to the body and there was blood everywhere. My unit went off to continue the mission, under the impression he was dead, knowing that it wasn't worth pressing the issue with our senior officers on the comms because, if he hadn't been killed, plenty of people would be working to keep him alive. *So what good would worrying do us?* Instead, we kept our concentration on the work ahead and once we'd returned to base the next day, our Officer Commanding gave us a full update.

'He's in bad shape,' the OC said. 'Several litres of blood have gone through him and the prognosis isn't great. The good news is he's alive and they're working to stabilize him. The bad news is his C2 vertebra has been disintegrated – his head has effectively been severed – so it'll be a life-changing injury for the lad.'

The news hit everyone hard, as it always did when somebody was seriously hurt or killed, but in those situations our only course of action was to control the controllable. I couldn't break down immediately or grieve fully because there was simply no time to reflect, not like there is in a civilian environment. The rhythm of conflict rarely afforded elite soldiers a chance to emotionally process death in that way because the enemy never allowed us to rest. There was no respite and we were constantly on alert. (It's important to understand that the processing of grief is contextual: I had to deal with it pragmatically because it was a part of my job. However, loss sometimes has the potential to become overwhelming. We'll talk about how to handle serious emotional trauma in Phase Eleven.)

Instead, we made sure to go through a brief period of respect at the time. If somebody was killed we took a moment to remember the good points over a 'wet' (the Royal Marines term for a brew). Before long, we'd be chatting about the funnier moments, where they'd screwed up or done something crazy or stupid, though it was always done with consideration and good intention. After that, we'd move on. There was no other choice. Any negative emotions towards the death such as sadness, anger, or even guilt, had to be tempered until an appropriate moment presented itself, such as when we returned home on leave or during a moment of national mourning, such as Remembrance Day, where everybody made a concerted effort to remember the lads that had been taken. That's when I'd make sure to fully process the loss, because to bottle it up any longer might prove destructive down the line.

This might sound emotionally unhealthy, but the alternative was to spin out of control, which wasn't an option. That's why death was never used by the senior command as a motivating factor on missions, especially in an environment where survival was tough enough. That style of management only caused an operator to work in a way that made life even riskier, though that's not to say it doesn't serve a purpose elsewhere. For example, in rugby, whenever a player is injured during a match, the remaining teammates might draw upon the incident at half time. It becomes fuel; using their colleague's pain becomes an inspirational force. *We're going to smash this lot because they've just fucked up one of our lads.* In those cases, turning anger into a positive energy is sometimes enough to ensure victory.

However, in war situations there's no place for that type of thinking. During a gunfight, I didn't have the room for anger or vengeful thought. An operator couldn't lose control or become reckless, taking out everybody in their way because a teammate had been shot. I had to manage my emotions. *And to do so it was important to rely upon self-awareness.* By understanding the thoughts and feelings that often kicked in during stressful situations, such as a gunfight, I was able to channel them effectively, with the three-step process. Firstly, I accepted and acknowledged the emotions: *I was scared, angry and stressed.* I then tried to understand why I was experiencing those feelings: *the enemy were firing at me and there was a chance I might get killed; one of my friends was dead.* Finally, I used those emotions to focus my actions: *I channelled fear, anger and stress in such a way that they helped me to concentrate on my next step.* People with anger management issues are unable to take those three steps, which is why they rarely make it into the military elite. In our line of work, where pride and professionalism are touchstones, there's no place for rage.

Don't get me wrong – I can be an angry person sometimes and my mates will probably testify to that. Every now and then I'll get wound up about things that should bounce off me, like a last-minute logistical change or an hour-long traffic jam. I suffered a serious sense-of-humour failure on the first day of Team Essence's Atlantic row as the coast of Lagos in Portugal faded into the distance and the inky black of night seemed to swallow up the boat. The initial adrenaline rush of what we'd embarked upon had worn off and everybody was readying themselves for the first shift of work: each individual was expected to do two hours on the oars followed by two hours of rest, for two brutal months.

'Let's get the hot wets on first,' I said, rubbing my hands. 'Someone get the coffee.'

Before our launch, each of us had been given a series of responsibilities to ready the boat for voyage. Former Royal Marine Ross Johnson was tasked with buying enough tea, coffee and hot chocolate to see us through the entire trip. As the crew readied for work, I noticed Ross bouncing around in the cabin, frantically scrabbling through our supplies. When he returned, his face was ashen.

'Er, lads,' he said nervously. 'I've left the brews behind.'

The rest of us were furious, me included, and for a minute I worried that somebody might launch Ross off the boat. But quickly we processed our emotions and resigned ourselves to the fact that there was nothing to drink but cold water for the next seven weeks (if we finished on time). Our combined military training had kicked in: *don't complain; find a solution*. And it was then accepted among the lads that we were all going to make at least one fuck-up each on the expedition, so it was for the best if we forgot about Ross's blunder and focused on working as a team – for now, at least. We could rinse him for it later.

That restraint was an instinct borne from combat. I don't remember ever feeling angry in a gunfight because there was zero room for negative emotion. I knew that to lose control would have resulted in me getting killed by the enemy. Acting irrationally was the fastest route to death. Instead of expressing anger, I became aggressive but in a controlled way. For example, if I'd helped to capture an enemy target in a raid, I usually worked to keep the captive under control. Then I advised my teammates to stay switched on.

'Right, keep the prisoner segregated. If he fucks around, sit him down hard, cuff him and let him know where he's at.'

I wasn't being a bully. The stress and adrenaline had risen within everybody, as it usually did in a situation of that nature. But if anything, controlled aggression helped to maintain a sense of calm because it convinced any detainees that the fight was over while ensuring that they didn't do anything stupid. Self-awareness turned our emotions into an asset.

But how do these theories work away from the theatre of combat or extreme adventure? Well, one way of gaining an increased sense of self-awareness is to recall a situation or two when our emotions have spiralled out of control, causing us to make a mistake in the fallout. Wouldn't it have been great if there had been an opportunity to acknowledge those feelings first, through self-awareness? The truth is that we can: *we're the peacekeepers for our reactions.* There will always be events that take place beyond our own influence. People will say things that upset us. Our best-laid plans will come under attack from an unexpected situational hand grenade. Usually there's nothing we can do to prevent those flashpoints from kicking off, but we can manage our responses in the aftermath. It just takes a little understanding, using the following three steps:

Step One: Thinking back to the 'Honesty About Self' first described in Phase Six, engage in some serious self-analysis regarding your strengths and weaknesses. Questions to ask yourself could include:

- Where are you most effective?
- Where do you tend to slip up?

- How do you react when under pressure?
- In what situations can others rely upon you?
- How do you behave in a time of crisis?
- When do you get angry, fearful, upset or feel emotionally out of control?

Step Two: Give these questions to your friends and colleagues, rewriting them so the questions are focused on you. Then steel yourself for some unpleasant responses. (To encourage a real beasting, ask your assessors to fill out the questions anonymously on a printout, rather than in a handwritten reply you might identify.)

Once those first two steps are completed, you'll have a clear picture of where to locate your emotional strengths as well as the events that can cause you to struggle.

Step Three: After any challenging event, gather your thoughts in a debrief session. Note how you reacted and list your actions, dividing them up into successes and mistakes. This process will give you an opportunity to understand the tactics that worked for you in certain scenarios and the ones that didn't. You'll soon receive a deeper understanding of your behaviour in scenarios such as flashpoints, moments of criticism, tests of self-confidence and high-pressure situations. A greater sense of self-awareness will follow. Equipped with that knowledge, you'll find it easy to understand the emotional chaos that can break out during difficult moments. Through understanding comes an acceptance that will lead to calmer thought. And with calmer thought, effective action is more easily achieved.

Soon you'll be able to control the controllable.

EMOTIONAL SELF-AWARENESS AND FOCUS

Internal focus is vital if we're to become more resilient. Too often on Selection for the Special Forces – and in any line of work, or a challenge, where a handful of people have to function alongside one another – individuals become distracted by how the people around them are doing. As a result, they lose focus on their own efforts and waste mental calories rather than directing their energy internally. Then they listen to the Demon chattering away, the voice telling them, 'If they can't do it, then you can't,' or 'They're so much better than you, mate. You can't keep up.' These internal distractions quickly derail the best of efforts.

In fairness, it's an easy pitfall to tumble into. As humans we have egos, which means we're psychologically hardwired to compare any successes or failures with the achievements of others. But this is a debilitating process because 1) It distracts us from the job in hand, 2) It can impact our confidence when finishing a task, and 3) Any comparisons to another individual could be based on misleading evidence. Sure, our cycling rival might be three kilometres ahead in the race, but maybe they're pacing themselves differently or struggling with an injury that might cause them to drop out. Instead, we should focus solely on ourselves and the intelligence available to us, without opinion or conjecture.

I'm all too familiar with the comparison trap because during my first day on the Briefing Phase that begins every Selection, I looked around at the other lads in my troop and started to stress.

Bloody hell, I thought, *there are some right monsters in here. I'm going to be up against it . . .*

I recognised soldiers I knew to be really talented. *Well, he's getting through, for sure*, I thought. *And him.*

But after a series of drills, which included a battle-swimming test comprising a timed, freestyle swim over 600 metres and a 25-metre underwater swim, I noticed that one or two formidable faces had dropped out. By the time we'd moved into the Hills Phase, our numbers had dwindled even more and some of the lads I'd imagined to be dead certs for the job were gone. I soon discovered that physical talent, while being incredibly important, wasn't the be-all and end-all when it came to Selection. Instead, resilience was the most highly prized attribute, and incredibly skilled soldiers often failed while the toughest clung on until the end.

It's a phenomenon we see a lot in professional sport, too. Great track and field athletes, or basketball players, can look the business when they first break through, but after a couple of seasons they fade away, often because they haven't got the fortitude or mindset to bounce back from an injury or a run of bad form. Meanwhile, competitors who might not have seemed too remarkable at the beginning of their careers end up winning major honours with a big team. They're viewed as being solid and reliable, but not amazing, and yet it's their grit that has enabled them to operate at the top level while more talented individuals have faded. When it came to my military career, I was that solid and reliable individual. I came to realize that while there were probably some better soldiers than me on my Selection course, I was a stubborn bastard who didn't like to fail. I prayed it would be enough to get me through.

As I threw myself into the long-distance runs on the Brecon Beacons during the Hills Phase, the middle of the pack became a familiar spot for me. I was never in any danger of finishing at the back but never too close to the front, either. I didn't let that bother me, though. I focused only on my own performance and what I needed to do in order to qualify for the next phase.

During the first week or so, whenever somebody dropped out around me, I used the resignation as emotional fuel. *They've flunked, but you're still hanging in there.* But the thought only lasted for a little while. Eventually, I gave up watching what was happening elsewhere altogether because I'd noticed some of the lads were being affected by the failures of others. It was as if they were thinking, *Bloody hell, if someone like him can't handle it, there's no way I'll be able to make it.* They were giving themselves permission to quit. Shortly afterwards they'd walk away, returning to their life in the Marines, their dream of making it as an elite soldier cut short.

We see it all the time on *SAS: Who Dares Wins.* During the first season, a mole was planted alongside the regular recruits. Ross Johnson (my forgetful teammate on the Atlantic crossing) had been a sturdy Royal Marine and he integrated with the other people in the civilian group as they worked through the various tests together. They were all oblivious to his secret past and a lot of the recruits in that season were looking at Ross as a possible winner. As far as they were concerned, he'd handled all the tests with ease and seemed to manage the physical and psychological challenges fairly comfortably. We'd decided during the latter stages that the Directing Staff would arrange a meeting where everybody was offered the chance to quit by handing in their armband. But, in a twist, we'd asked Ross to drop out at that same point. We'd wanted to see what effect him quitting would have on the others. *Which recruits had the internal focus to stay switched on regardless?* Unsurprisingly, when Ross handed over his armband, a couple of his fellow recruits dropped out moments later.

Truly, the only people that make it to the end of *SAS: Who Dares Wins* are those team players capable of maintaining internal focus. Don't get me wrong – I'll still fall victim to diversions from time to time. I might compare myself with the imagined strength of the individuals around me; we each have an ego, after all. Occasionally, I'll get into the gym and work out with someone I haven't met before, a lad who looks mega-strong.

Fucking hell, I'll think. *I could embarrass myself here.*

But I'll soon recognize the Demon. Working hard to shut it up, I'll press ahead, thinking, *Sod it, I'll get on with the work.* Nine times out of ten the other person burns themselves out long before I've finished the session. They quit, but I'm still grinding on, focusing only on what I have to do to get to where I need to be.

EMOTIONAL SELF-AWARENESS AND FLEXIBILITY

Life on military tour was a roller coaster of emotion.

My brain was constantly being exposed to stresses and strains, and the Demon liked popping up whenever I felt frazzled. For example, during the time spent walking to an operation I would often be wracked with anticipation and feel a little anxious, especially if my nerves had been frayed by fatigue after weeks and weeks of night raids. Even when I wasn't working, I was expected to train every day at the gym on base, which comprised a sandblasted collection of weights and racks. The effort was physically tough because we didn't take it easy. Everybody in the squadron was often knackered and the only way to cope with the mental turbulence was through self-awareness and flexibility.

Anything could happen, so I had to be ready for anything happening.

I wasn't constantly trying to predict any awful eventuality that might take place. Rather, I was always mentally ready for plans to change, and at short notice. There was no way an operator could function with rigid thought; routine didn't exist at the sharp end of war, and without flexibility an elite soldier would emotionally snap in half because the job was in a constant state of flux. Nowhere was this idea more stress-tested than in the build-up to missions, when we gathered in the mess, each of us ready to grab our night-vision goggles, scrapping gear and shock-and-awe weaponry if the order came. While we waited for instructions, we'd sometimes sit around the telly to watch whatever football game was going on back in England. Some of the lads might play darts, others cards; all of us anticipating the call to action from a telephone that linked the mess to our Officer Commanding. The mood was usually tense and uncertain. *Is it going to kick off tonight? Or are we being stood down?*

Whenever the phone rang, the lads looked at one another expectantly.

'Get the phone, then!' someone would shout.

'You fucking get it, you're right there!'

There would be a moment or two of bickering before the nearest operator reluctantly grabbed at the receiver, entirely aware the room was hanging on their reaction.

'Yeah? Right. Yeah, roger that.'

He'd then sit down, behaving as if nothing had happened.

Well?

'What? Oh yeah! The mission's been shit-canned. We're not going out.'

Sometimes jobs were cancelled because of bad weather. At other times, our transport might unexpectedly need servicing – relying on mechanical equipment in a desert was occasionally problematic. Disruption happened the other way round, too. Sometimes we had settled down to eat, only to be upended because a high-profile target was suddenly within reach or about to launch an attack. But living in an out-of-control environment was part of the job, so flexibility soon became a vital tool in levelling out the stress. I knew there was no point worrying about what bad stuff might, or might not, happen once the work began for real. That was the first step towards becoming a nervous wreck, because so many things could go wrong on missions.

The helicopter might crash.

A mate might get shot.

I might die, or suffer a life-changing injury.

Sure, all of those things *might* happen. On the other hand, they might not. So, in the same way that it wasn't worth lying in my bunk at night worrying about what could happen if I were to get really sick, lose my job, crash the car or split up with my significant other, it wasn't worth worrying about what might happen if I were to step on an IED or if a mission went horribly wrong. Because missions went horribly wrong all the time. The only rational course of action was to plan as much as I could and stay flexible, ready for any change. It was the only way I could prepare for a job that had a tendency to go south at any given moment.

Try considering this emotional position for any challenge in life: *Anything can happen, so remain adaptable.* The alternative is to live in a constant state of shock. And nobody can function effectively in that environment.

EMOTIONAL SELF-AWARENESS, JUVENILE THOUGHT AND THE IMPORTANCE OF THINKING LIKE A KID

So, how does an individual truly locate that relaxed state of mind?

In the military elite we were trained to be flexible and for large chunks of my career I was able to live in the moment, rather than focusing upon what was taking place in the next ten minutes or what had happened ten minutes previously. That allowed me to be calm and responsive no matter what was going on around me. In that respect, I found that some elite soldiers were, weirdly, quite Zen in their outlook on life. (I even know of ex-operators who have been described as 'hippies', which also seems a bit weird.) But as a brotherhood we were able to roll with the punches whenever life became scrappy or stressful, because we understood the power of remaining flexible and positive. In tense moments we used self-awareness to appreciate our survival; we made jokes and killed time by playing cards or training in the gym, because the awful reality was that we might have already been dead had fate taken the enemy's side in the last scrap and not ours.

While the idea of living in the moment may sound simple when written down in a book, in practice it can take a fair amount of effort. I'd learned about that mindset as a teenager because it had been drummed into every Royal Marines Commando at Lympstone. We were taught to be malleable, to think on our feet and to adopt a positive attitude at all times. (I think it was a position I took to naturally anyway.) However, once I'd been medically discharged from the military at the end of my career, that mental strength faded away. Due to the onset of PTSD, I'd already become fearful of what might happen to me in a gunfight. Once in the Real World I found myself being hyper-vigilant during moments of crisis, such as a dispute at home or a problem at work. My self-awareness and flexibility waned and I fell apart.

But I was able to grab it back. One of the first breakthroughs in reclaiming my sense of self took place during therapy, when I learned why my resilience had deteriorated so drastically throughout that fateful, final military tour. I realized that when I was a younger bloke, pushing through Selection and operating as an elite soldier, I rarely considered the dangerous implications of what I was doing. If I was about to swoop into a terrorist camp or raid an enemy munitions dump, I just did it. I didn't overthink the plan – or the risks. I lived in the now. That made me impervious to stress and fear. As I got older, however, I analysed the threats to my life a little more. I think it's something we all do with age – we become more cautious, and the sort of things we once did without stress as younger people eventually prey on our mind more intensely. In the aftershocks of conflict during my final tour, I'd allowed those concerns to overcome me.

One suggestion for helping me to push forward was to think in a more juvenile way. The first step was to stop overanalysing my actions, which I hadn't done during my early career, and to do so I'd need to look at life in a childlike way. Most two-year-olds will waddle into a room of other kids their age and mix easily. They won't question intentions or make assumptions about anyone around them. All they want to do is play, and any associated risk to their well-being seems irrelevant. Ordinarily, the consequences of something that might have happened earlier that day won't play on their mind; nor will the events of the coming afternoon. Sure, they'll have tantrums, but they'll be forgotten within minutes, and most of the time kids generally explore life without too much stress. They're strangely self-aware too: most kids know what makes them happy and what causes them to become sad. Therapy encouraged me to think in the same way. I was asked to let go of any judgements about my past and forget the fears for my future. I had to tap into what made me happy rather than what made me fearful. It took a little while to get into the idea, but it was worth it once I did.

Philosophers and therapists have long encouraged people to think like children – to act with the bare minimum of analysis, self-imposed pressure or trepidation. Zen Buddhists call it the Beginner's Mind, a state of thinking where an individual is completely without fear, open to new experiences and living in the moment. I've used the concept when working through different therapeutic methods for PTSD because if we're able to think like children in negative moments, then we're able to free any situations from our prejudgement or anticipation. Instead, we can assess situations more clearly and push past any physical or psychological barriers.

I've often put that process to the test, with successful results. In 2018 I had a meeting with a production team from Channel Four where I was asked a fairly simple question: 'If you could go anywhere to make a documentary, where would it be?' At that time, I had no doubt in my mind. I wanted to return to Afghanistan, the scene of some of the most horrific episodes in my life, and the place where I'd first started to emotionally unravel. (With hindsight I should have suggested the Maldives.) By 2019 I'd been commissioned to make *Foxy's War*, an hour-long documentary on Afghanistan, though I wasn't entirely sure what I was hoping to report on once I'd got there – as far as the film-making went, my brief was pretty open-ended, but I was happy to roll with it.

Nevertheless, I definitely became worried in the weeks building up to my return. I wasn't that bothered about seeing something that might upset me; I'd come to terms with my PTSD experience and felt emotionally steady. But I was nervous about getting hurt. Afghanistan was still a very sketchy place. I wasn't ready to die and I knew that my chances of copping it were greatly increased by returning. At first, I stressed.

As the days counted down to my trip, I hoped that Channel Four would have second thoughts, or that somebody high up might decide the project was too risky or too stupid. But, despite my fears, there was no way I was backing out of the project myself: I'd agreed to do it so I was going to follow through with the job. However, the situation reminded me of a nervy moment in the weeks building up to the Atlantic row with Team Essence. I'd gone to Ibiza for a break, and as I stared out across the water one night I became unsettled. I pictured our boat rowing away from land, into darkness, the team drifting from civilization – maybe for good. It was quite a daunting thought.

Afghanistan gave me the same chill.

That's when I decided to bring myself into the now, to think like a kid again. So, I took the following two steps:

- I acknowledged the negative experiences I'd gone through in the past and reminded myself that I'd survived them, thanks to my training. I should forget those negative experiences for now.
- I told myself that there was no point in worrying about any awful incidents that *might* happen during filming and I used my therapy to rationalize any fear for the future. *Of course I was worried! I was going back to one of the most dangerous places on earth.* It was a normal fear and should be respected. But there was also every chance that nothing bad would take place. Rather than knackering myself out through stress, I needed to react to dangerous moments only if they kicked off, while being flexible enough to respond.

Meanwhile, I used the negative emotion to switch on; I became more focused, as I had in the military. *Being scared was a good thing.* I was out of my comfort zone again, learning and growing, which meant I was becoming more resilient. One thing I've realized is that, as much as we like having comfortable lives (and I wouldn't be unhappy if I were to have a totally comfortable life from now on), if I'm to grow I need to put myself in uncomfortable situations. It's one of the reasons why I've kept doing *SAS: Who Dares Wins.* Every time another season has been announced, I've mentally prepared myself for the work to come, knowing that a series of psychological challenges are going to be chucked my way, such as jumping from that way-too-high diving platform. But once I've arrived on the job and thrown myself into an intense situation or two, I've become pretty happy, self-aware and comfortable in the uncomfortable. I've then experienced growth.

Filming in Afghanistan was the same. There were troubling moments, for sure, but I worked through them with a juvenile attitude – I lived only in the now, rather than worrying about what had happened there while we'd been preparing for our trip (there had been reports of suicide bombs) or what might take place once I arrived (I knew that, as a former elite soldier and a TV journalist, I presented a high-profile target, with plenty of kudos for an enemy force looking to kill or capture a Westerner). By focusing on the moment, I was able to deal with any risks or flashpoints calmly and with purpose, but only when they occurred. By working without irrational fear, I was able to operate effectively. As a result, my chances of survival became far greater than if I'd been an anxious, stressed-out bag of shit, and

I only allowed myself to really consider the danger I'd been in once I'd returned home. By then I was safe and sound. All the drama was over.

I was so glad I went. While travelling across Afghanistan, I realized that I both loved and loathed the country. I suppose that sense of a pending discovery was what triggered my suggestion in the first place. During military tours, I'd enjoyed the way the country had looked, and some of the people were amazing (though there were definitely some less-than-amazing individuals living there, too). The atmosphere and culture in the less conflicted corners of the country were also interesting, and as I worked with the film crew I developed a weird understanding about myself. This will sound strange, but maybe I'd loved the war. I certainly thrived in the chaos, because that's what I'd been trained for. I also buzzed off the purpose the work had once given me, because I'd believed we were striving for a better future in Afghanistan while protecting the people we cared for at home from terrorist attacks. What did I loathe? The violence; death. So, there was a lot of sadness that went hand in hand with the positives when I explored Afghanistan again. But maybe that balance is what being a human is all about. I was drawn to Afghanistan because it gave me such a mix of emotions.

Overall, though, I'd wanted to know that my work with the British Armed Forces had been *for something*; confirmation that I'd also made a good job of it would have been nice as well. Despite all the political arguments debating the rights and wrongs of conflicts of that nature, some positives had come out of the War on Terror, and when I travelled across

Afghanistan I realized that my work had indeed been constructive. For example, we'd trained up a competent local fighting force, lads who were working to defend their country from some very unpleasant aggressors. Their hope was to secure a positive future for Afghanistan. But it was also great to see that the world had changed for a lot of the women living in the region. Under the Taliban's old rules, women had been oppressed and many of them were treated terribly, but when I returned I met with groups of women who had started striving for independence. They were taking on physical challenges that would have been unimaginable twenty years previously because they wouldn't have been allowed to participate in them. As we showed at the close of *Foxy's War*, I even went trekking with a group of female adventurers who had decided they were going to explore the country's wilder areas, and they were scaling pretty gnarly terrain. One member of the group had even climbed the tallest peaks in Afghanistan and was now highly skilled when surviving on the mountains alone for long periods of time. It was a silver lining to a war that had felt quite bleak at times.

In the end I used the film as a platform to show people the results of the British Armed Forces' efforts. The viewers could then make up their own minds as to whether the conflict had been worth it or not.

To round up: when managing our demons it's important to remember that an emotional experience can accompany any number of events where sacrifice or suffering takes place – and self-awareness can help us to regain control. For example, it might be that we need to undergo an important surgical procedure. The weeks building up to the appointment can be filled with dread. We stress about what might happen during the operation and fear for the consequences should something go wrong. The key to overcoming those fears is to acknowledge their root cause. *Of course it's a worrying situation! Surgery is an invasive and intimidating experience.* During these moments of negativity, it's important to focus on the now – we should tell ourselves to consider a negative event only if it actually happens.

Just as my time in Afghanistan was unsettling occasionally, hospital visits and surgery can be loaded with anxious moments, especially if our life is under threat. But by living only in the now, it's possible to manage those scary flashpoints. And once the trauma has healed, weeks and months down the line, the benefits of enduring such a difficult event can be revealed. Sometimes those benefits are even life-changing.

OPERATIONAL DEBRIEF

» Negative emotions are early warning signals: they tell us when something is wrong, even though we might not realize it. How we react to them is completely within our control, even though the situation that caused them might not be. We should first acknowledge the presence of fear, grief, anger, guilt and other feelings. It's then important to understand why they've appeared and to manage their impact.

» We should accept our emotional weaknesses rather than pretend they don't exist. From there we can reduce their negative influence by working to overcome them. Failing that, we can find a way to circumnavigate their effects.

» To get a greater sense of self-awareness, ask some tough questions of yourself. For a more thorough examination, ask others to answer those questions about you as well. Steel yourself for a pretty rough ride, but the process will give you more tactical intelligence as a result.

» Internal focus is vital when becoming resilient. Too often we allow negative external forces to affect us. Never judge your performance by the successes or failures of others. Instead, use those mental calories to concentrate on your own work.

» Learn to become flexible by living in the now. Focus on the immediate seconds and metres ahead rather than being stressed out by past events or what might happen in the future. We can only control the controllable.

SITUATIONAL AWARENESS

IT'S OK TO NOT FEEL OK

Everybody feels shit from time to time. We can wake up in a foul mood and not know why, or feel crushed by whatever's been going on in life to the point where we emotionally spin out. It's sometimes hard to feel like anything's within our control. The trick to regaining a sense of power is to acknowledge the humanity of our situation with honesty: despite the slogans from a million ad campaigns, *it's OK to not feel great.* Life isn't one endless success story and it's a positive step if we decide to approach any unfortunate circumstances with honesty and self-awareness, rather than trying to convince ourselves that everything's fine. However, it *isn't* OK if we don't attempt to bring a level of positivity into our thinking as we go forward.

There are countless times when I could have been overwhelmed by negative thoughts during war. Sometimes an enemy might have taken the upper hand in a scrap, and I saw the horrific impact hostile militia forces were having on peaceful communities. Whenever I experienced an emotional crash, I acknowledged the negative emotions I was feeling. I then searched for the root cause. Had I ignored whatever was troubling me it probably would have festered to the point where I'd forgotten what had triggered it in the first place. Unable to figure out what was really wrong, I'd have found myself in serious trouble. In the end, I forgot my own tried-and-tested practices and that led to my breakdown, but I've since relearned how to correct an emotional tailspin.

As I've said, part of the issue when leaving the military was that I didn't face up to my problems as I had in the past. I couldn't acknowledge that I was feeling shame, fear, resentment, guilt and anger. I pretended I was OK and in frustration I'd sometimes explode with rage over the smallest thing. Had I been honest with myself, I could have tackled the issues a lot sooner; I'd have been able to draw some positives from my situation. It would have been possible to discover a sense of clarity long before things had become so desperate.

I've since learned that being negative is tiring. I fuck up all the time, but I try to turn those fuck-ups into constructive thought. Some mornings I'll wake up in a bad mood that I can't shake off, but whenever I've felt myself slumping like this, I remember the advice we've given to lads at Rock2Recovery when they come in for the first time: *always try to find a positive, no matter how small*. It's not always easy, but once the technique becomes habitual it can have a transformative effect, even in the most extreme situations, for example:

#1 At rock bottom, I decided there was nowhere else to go but up.

#2 In therapy, I reassured myself that I was getting help from people who could save me.

#3 While being shot at, I told myself that at least I wasn't dead – yet.

I'm lucky to have built that level of self-awareness over time. Sadly, too many people seem unwilling to analyse themselves when dealing with some of the more serious issues in their lives. They rarely accept the shit they're feeling. They ignore negativity; they pretend to the people around them that everything's OK because to do otherwise makes them feel embarrassed or like a failure, so their pain gradually increases, like toothache. But this happens on a micro level too. I can walk around all day and see negative emotion written all over the faces of some people. They're angry. They behave ignorantly. They act irrationally or unpredictably. For a lot of those individuals, their day has begun badly – they've woken up feeling crap about something or had an argument with their partner – and it's sent them into a spiral. Having stormed out of the house, they've then ignored the rules of basic psychological admin: accept, understand, resolve.

That sounds overly simple, doesn't it? But with even the smallest shred of self-awareness it's possible to shift a negative mindset to something more positive, and reasonably quickly. (That's why the idea of having *one of those days* is a concept that does my head in. It's nonsense.) *The first step is to prevent the Demon from taking hold.* No matter what went wrong in the first place, understand that a bad start is not the sign of an impending run of bad luck. Wallowing in pessimism is a grim mindset to adopt, especially in a crisis, where negative thought and self-pity can lead an individual to make poor decisions, which then increases the potential danger in a situation.

The next step is to take positive action. I might smash my toe on a sharp corner as I get out of bed, accidentally break something in the house or have a dispute with someone I care for or work with. There's no point dwelling on the incident. Instead, I follow the three rules of basic psychological admin, and then press ahead. At no point do I let the Demon in, or think, *Shit, it's going to be a rough day. Everything's going against me*, because that thought process is self-destructive and debilitating. Instead, I'll give myself an emotional pep talk: *You have to get rid of that moment. Put it down to being a one-off and the rest of the day will be brilliant.* I'll then repeat it, over and over, until I feel on an even keel again.

Finally, I'll reaffirm my positive mindset with an unfuck-upable action. I'll make a cup of tea, perform some simple work or smash through a gym session using my success in that area as evidence that the bad event of the morning was nothing but a one-off.

Right, the day's not against me, I think. *On we go.*

It might sound like hocus-pocus, but as a self-correcting measure it's been pretty effective so far.

PART TWO

BY STRENGTH AND GUILE

AUTHOR'S NOTE

No amount of battle prep in the world can ready a soldier 100 per cent for their first gunfight (although it comes really close). The same goes for firefighters and house blazes, police officers and drug busts, paramedics and 999 calls. Creating an environment where an individual is able to experience a little of the mortal threat that might take place on the job is important, but nobody wants to kill potential service crew during development.

In the case of my military experience, Selection definitely provided me with a psychological framework for survival. Training then gave me the skills required to cope with conflict; I was given insight into the challenges ahead and the mechanisms for dealing with any unusual events. But at the back of the brain there was always a disclaimer that said, *I'm not really going to get shot here.*

I waited ages for my first battle. I spent weeks on military tour hoping for the fighting to begin, but when the first scrap finally started, my mentality changed in a heartbeat and I remember thinking, *Oh shit – actually, I didn't really want this to happen* . . . Then my adrenaline soared; I went into a weird trance where everything seemed to happen instinctively. My training had kicked in and I was able to function without fear or self-doubt. I'd been provided with all the procedures for operating under extreme pressure.

Part One of *Life Under Fire* has acted in pretty much the same way – it has instilled the skills required to thrive in moments of high stress or during gruelling life-events. But now the work begins for real. Over the coming chapters, I'll deliver the necessary intel on how to cope fully with your first battle, whatever that might be. You'll learn how to prepare for missions and what to do when the metaphorical shooting kicks off. We'll discuss how to react when the odds are stacked against your challenge or when you've been incapacitated and it feels as if you can't press ahead without reinforcements. Finally, I'll explain how the military elite maximizes victory and minimizes defeat, ensuring we remain robust enough to push on to our next mission, no matter how hard the enemy tries to derail us.

Thanks to Part One, you already have the Battle Mind. Now you'll be able to apply that resilient thought by working to the motto of the Special Boat Service: By Strength and Guile.

PHASE EIGHT

MISSION PLANNING:
PREPPING FOR PAIN

In military life, preparation is everything.

The shortest route to casualties and hard lessons is to engage with a highly motivated and dangerous enemy in an unpredictable theatre of conflict without a plan. This applies to just about every challenge in life. Entering a project or event without preparation or research is foolhardy and should be avoided at all costs.

To emphasize this idea, it's worth noting that a large number of deaths occur on mountain treks simply because the participants haven't understood some of the risks associated with the environment. In 2015, a total of thirty hillwalkers died in the Lake District, an area that's considered to be fairly benign by most people. But without suitable training, the right equipment and a period of preparation, a person can push too hard in what might have initially seemed like an innocuous activity. As an example of what can happen during any unplanned challenge, this is about as apt as any.

In war, mission planning takes place in a variety of ways.

Sometimes operations will have been based on months of intelligence-gathering and strategic analysis. On other occasions, such as when an unexpected event or attack has occurred, we've had to react quickly, rather than working in a methodical and proactive fashion. I've even been on jobs where the planning detail was scribbled down on a ripped-open cigarette packet while speeding towards our target in a helicopter. It might have felt rushed, but at least some semblance of tactical structure was in place.

As I've stated previously, 'No plan survives contact.' But if a mission is built on solid intelligence and effective strategy then it has a greater chance of overcoming the biggest of hurdles.

MISSION-PLAN LIKE AN ELITE OPERATOR

By working through Part One of the book, a clearer understanding of your 'why' might have already arrived; at the very least, one or two ideas are hopefully bubbling up. Maybe you've thought about cracking on with a start-up project or developing a new business idea. Perhaps you're entering into a series of 10K races around Europe or considering an extreme trek, such as Mount Kilimanjaro or the Welsh 3000s challenge (a 24-hour yomp across the fourteen 3,000-metre peaks in Snowdonia). Or it could be that a life-change is now in the offing: a house move, a wedding or the decision to start a family. All of these purposes are both exciting and challenging, and to ensure that you remain resilient throughout whatever it is you're doing next, it's important to first recall the five components of resilience – purpose, experience, brotherhood, honesty and self-awareness – and to then create a serious course of action, aka the *Mission Plan*.

In Special Forces settings, mission plans happened in one of two ways. The first was proactive: a detailed course of action built on weeks or months of intelligence-gathering and preparation. The second was reactive: the stressful, seat-of-the-pants job, when things kicked off unexpectedly and usually at the worst possible moment. These events required us to think on our feet, rather than prepare methodically in advance, so we'll focus on the more considered approach because, hopefully, there's plenty of time for you to plan your next challenge.

Having built up a clear picture of the target, or targets, that our squadron was set to engage with, a solid battle plan was laid out to the units involved in a detailed, step-by-step briefing. Most operations were structured in this way because it gave every individual involved a clear idea of their roles and responsibilities. The steps were as follows:

Prelims: A basic introduction to the situation around us. In broad strokes we were told what the enemy what was up to. *What intelligence did we have on them?* There was an update on what our forces were doing. Then we discussed what we would do were we to be attacked during the briefing. We were also briefed on first light, last light and even the moon state. *Was it waxing or waning?*

As part of the Prelims, we discussed the **Ground**. This was an insight into the area we were moving into and the buildings or terrain we were likely to encounter. *The hostage is being held in a* *heavily protected compound in the middle of a small village on the edge of the mountains.*

Situation: Detail on the enemy forces in the area, the assets at their disposal and the kind of resistance we could expect to face. *The enemy are a highly motivated group and well armed. They tend to defend aggressively. Expect strong resistance.* Our available resources were also detailed, such as the number of supporting troops involved in the mission and any air assets we could call upon.

Mission: The objective of the job was spelled out in plain and simple terms. *The mission tonight is to rescue the hostage.* For clarity, the objective was then repeated to the group. *The mission tonight is to rescue the hostage.*

Execution: The basic plan. During this process, everybody was given instructions of what to do on the ground. The group was split into teams, or units. Each team had a specific task to concentrate on and execute.

Command and Signals: In short, who's in charge? How do we communicate? And what code words are in operation? For example: Jackpot = *Job done.*

On paper, this probably appears to be an overwhelming process. Certainly, for the operators involved these mission-planning sessions could last for up to three hours, but I was always far happier tackling a dangerous mission having been forewarned with exhaustive instructions. The alternative was to be blindsided by an unexpected event when working on the ground.

What's great about the British military's mission-planning process is that it can be applied to any project that requires physical and mental fortitude. To illustrate this, I'll frame the process through the lens of our aforementioned mountain trek. For the purposes of a non-military mission, where it's probably not important to have a contingency plan in case of an enemy attack during the Prelims, I've tweaked the structure ever so slightly.

MOUNT KILIMANJARO EXPEDITION

Prelims: What's the situation? 'I need to challenge myself mentally and physically. I thrive outdoors and I want to raise money for a cause that's close to my heart. I have plenty of holiday time coming up, so I'm organizing a group trip to climb Mount Kilimanjaro for charity.'

Ground: The trek will take five to nine days to complete. It's a 'walk-up' mountain so no technical climbing skills will be required, but the summit is 5,895 metres high so altitude will be a factor.

Situation: Be ready for altitude sickness – headaches, nausea, shortness of breath and fatigue. The walk is set to be a physical challenge. Mentally, there will be periods of fear and self-doubt.

Mission: Spell it out in plain and simple terms. *The mission is to summit Mount Kilimanjaro for charity.* Then repeat. *The mission is to summit Mount Kilimanjaro for charity.*

Execution: The basic plan for climbing Mount Kilimanjaro: the trekking schedule and miles walked per day; meals and accommodation details; required equipment. Always consider your *What if*s. Assign roles should something go wrong, such as an injury on the mountain.

Command and Signals: This should include details on the expedition company, the guides leading the group and their support staff. Contact details for everyone on the trip should be consolidated on to one WhatsApp group for smoother communications. Emergency numbers should be distributed in case of a *What if* event.

When placed in a non-military context, this process seems fairly straightforward. Utilizing this style of battle order will help you through your next challenge. For example, if you're planning to open up a new company, use a mission plan to figure out the final idea, ideal office location, potential obstacles, financial infrastructure, legal requirements and how to communicate your new idea to the market. The alternative is to be unprepared, which is never an ideal spot to be in, either in or out of war.

It's important to point out that during my time with the military, dangerous missions took place at short notice all the time – which was where that ripped-open cigarette packet sometimes came in handy – but we were never dispatched on one without some explanation as to why we were about to risk our lives; the ultimate objectives were always stated to the group involved, no matter how quickly we had to execute them. Our goal and relevant motives for an assault were always shouted out prior to us landing on an enemy compound or seeking out a high-profile target in a hard arrest. For example:

#1 'We're seeking Target X because he's an IED facilitator responsible for a number of suicide bombs that have been set off in the area.'

#2 'We're walking on to Area X because we believe there's a weapons stockpile hidden there.'

Details of this kind helped to bring clarity and resilience to an operator as they worked under pressure. When the shooting started, it always helped to have a clear idea of the job that we were working on and how it fed into the overall goals of the British military. Having left the Special Forces it's a trick I've since used in all sorts of tasks.

I'm doing this honking run because I need to stay expedition-fit.

I'm going into this meeting because it might create a business opportunity for me down the line.

That's not to say my resolve isn't occasionally challenged when working through a mission plan, but with a clear under-standing of the whats, whys and hows of a mission, I can prepare for those tricky events more effectively, with a sharper focus. The dark thoughts and low moments pass by easily.

IN MISSION PLANNING, INTEL IS EVERYTHING

In war, the success of every mission hinges on intelligence – the information regarding each and every aspect of an operation, which may or may not include location, the enemy on the ground, their capabilities, any assets at their disposal, the presence of a person of interest, our best time to attack, weather conditions, and so on. Prior to any job, it was the role of the squadron to gather together as much knowledge as possible in order to build a 360-degree picture of the challenges ahead. And it's vital to do the same in any project requiring a modicum of resilience.

Generally, military intelligence was categorized in three ways:

- Human intelligence: information gathered by chatting to locals in a hostile area, from eyewitness accounts or from informants.
- Airborne intelligence: knowledge obtained through drones, spy planes or assets patrolling over an area of interest.
- Signal intelligence: the dark arts of spying, such as wiretaps, hacking or other cyber weapons.

#1 Human Intelligence
There were a number of times as an operator where I was required to enter enemy territory in order to meet with a contact

or snitch. These sources were known as human intelligence – people who for one reason or another had decided to help the British military, and whose role was to provide updates on any individuals or places of interest. Human intelligence is the oldest method of collecting information, and until the technical revolution of the mid to late twentieth century, it was the primary source of intelligence.

Human intelligence is vital to anyone embarking on a challenge or life-event. In order to detail how intelligence-gathering works and how it can be applied to a non-military operation, I'll use the example of a family who are planning to relocate to another country. This can be an incredibly stressful and time-consuming effort; all sorts of hoops have to be jumped through and human intelligence is essential. For starters, it's always smart to appoint an immigration lawyer with a good reputation. It also helps to contact people who have experienced moving from one country to another in order to build a picture of what to expect and how best to prepare for the challenges ahead. These might sound like basic suggestions, but you'd be surprised at the number of people who fail to do their homework. They apply for an unsuitable visa, fail to understand the cultural differences when buying a house abroad, and misjudge the amount of time a procedure of this kind requires. It's easy to be crushed by the process as a result, but some serious bother can be saved with even the most basic level of intelligence-gathering. As the Special Forces teaches everybody: to be an elite soldier it's important to execute the basics very, very well.

#2 Airborne Intelligence

A huge amount of modern warfare is conducted from the air. Drones are used in airspaces all over the world to track enemy forces and criminals (it's not only in the theatre of conflict that they're utilized to gain the upper hand) and I often worked with air assets on a military tour. With their help, it was possible to build up a picture of how an enemy target operated, from a safe distance. Most days I would watch hostile figures going about their day-to-day business, unaware they were being spied upon by eyes far above them. We were able to watch and understand their activities, allowing us to plan our next course of action. As with any observation post, every movement by the target was noted down in a factual manner; there was no room for speculation or guesswork.

At this point you might be wondering, *How does aerial intelligence help somebody to emigrate?* Or, *What the bloody hell has this got to do with my plans to run a marathon?* But think of aerial intelligence as visual detail. Sure, you're running a long-distance race, but what does that event look like? All races are different. The London Marathon, for example, is a relatively flat course. But New York is a slow climb; there are several bridges to deal with, too, and the last couple of miles take place over the undulating terrain of Central Park. It helps to be forewarned of those particular challenges. Likewise our hypothetical move abroad: what will our new lifestyle look like? It's all very well having an idyllic image in our heads, but the reality will probably be very different, so a reconnaissance mission should be conducted. Building a clear sense of how the experience actually appears, and what challenges it might bring, is vital when hoping to avoid any nasty shocks on the ground.

#3 Signal Intelligence

The nature of signal intelligence-gathering is almost unrecognizable from when I first started life as a Royal Marines Commando. These days, email accounts are hacked from remote sources, viruses are planted into online comms systems and information is extracted remotely. That's beyond my remit. I merely relied on the signal intelligence that was gathered by foraging techniques, so I couldn't tell you exactly how the gathering process worked or when it was utilized (nor would I want to, because the Ministry of Defence would have my balls in a vice). What I can tell you is that signal intelligence was incredibly useful, especially when trying to build a picture of how the enemy was operating.

Technology is now a part of everyone's life – it's not only the British military that get to build a picture of their forthcoming challenges through smartphones and online assets. We all have the ability to research and learn from the resources at our fingertips. Someone suffering from a serious illness can search the internet for the best method of self-care or look into online counselling. The novice Ironman Triathlon athlete can read about the experiences of competitors who have previously taken part in the event. From there they can understand the value of race management, rehydration, energy gels and why it's important to shove an Imodium tablet into their pocket before leaving home. (Spoiler: to avoid an uncomfortable episode of diarrhoea halfway round.) For just about every gruelling experience in life, someone has now either blogged about it, produced a podcast on the subject or written an Instagram post. It makes sense to tap into that intel.

MISSION PLANNING
AND EMOTIONAL CHAOS

Negative emotions have the potential to overwhelm us during any mission. It might be that we're preparing to do something unpleasant in our work life, such as firing a colleague we feel close to. A house move will require us to say goodbye to some close friends and neighbours. In other cases, there may be an event looming on the horizon that taps into our greatest fears, like a physical challenge involving heights or speed, or a requirement to speak in front of hundreds of people or motivate a room full of strangers.

We may have to ready ourselves for events when we can expect to feel physical pain: physiotherapy or root canal surgery are good examples. Elsewhere, we may become angry, sad or scared, or feel guilty or stressed depending on the situation we're going through. But we can prepare for all these moments by adjusting for negative thought within the mission plan, predicting our reactions and then compartmentalizing our fears for when they actually arrive, worrying about them only if we need to.

Whenever I was going into a dust-up within the military, I always prepared myself psychologically by briefly running through some of the things I could expect to see along the way.

Right, we're going into a badass place, I'd tell myself. *We're probably going to have to kill a few people. I'm going to see some fucked-up stuff and there's likely to be a lot of explosions and other crazy shit.*

The process readied me, but I didn't dwell on it – as I've stated before, there's no point frazzling our adrenal systems by fretting over the many *What ifs* in life. Sure enough, when explosions, shootings and 'fucked-up stuff' happened, I wasn't completely unsettled. Mentally, I was already prepared.

I've since used that mission-planning technique in my civilian work. When working on the TV show *Meet the Drug Lords: Inside the Real Narcos* I was thrown into a series of sketchy situations, some of which could have upended me emotionally, had I not been primed. At one point, I went into a *barrio* in Colombia to meet a couple of narco dudes who were known to be incredibly dangerous. The area was lawless. I'd been told that it was a total no-go location and that undercover police were unable to work there, such was its notoriety. The buildings were shacks set on stilts, and armed gangs lurked on street corners. Even during daylight, the *barrio* had an unnerving vibe. *Bad things happened there.*

We hadn't helped ourselves, dressing in tabards like non-governmental-organization workers, and from the minute we arrived for our meeting the locals pointed and stared. Lads made gun signs and pretended to shoot us – clearly we weren't being welcomed with open arms. (All of us were equipped with hidden cameras; had they been discovered we definitely would have been executed.) When the news came through that our meeting had been delayed, we had to hide out in a shack. I told the cameraman to stand away from the window because there was every chance somebody might decide to open fire on our position. But I was able to stay calm because I'd briefly readied myself for what we could expect on the ground. As I had done before most military operations, I'd assessed the situation and its potential for danger during a mission plan. *I'm going into a scary place, unarmed. There will be people with guns who will hate us being there, and they will try to intimidate the group. And there is every chance it could kick off and we might have to run for it.* By the time our interview eventually took place, I felt emotionally steady – well, as steady as a person can be when a mob of heavily armed cartel *capos* have entered the room.

That kind of stress hits me in non-violent situations, too. I've often given talks to corporate groups wanting to learn from my experiences in conflict. After all, knowing how to manage stress in a high-pressure situation is a valuable tool in any industry. (A technique for managing stressful situations such as public speaking is detailed later on in this chapter.) I usually feel fairly confident in my delivery, having now done hundreds of presentations, but last year I was asked to record a podcast in front of a live studio audience in a London pub. The idea unsettled me a little. I'd fronted podcasts before, recording a series of interviews with people who had shown resilience in challenging situations. However, for the live event, I was asked to interview the bushcraft, mountaineering and climbing guide Megan Hine. Alongside her was James Ketchell, who had previously made his name by completing the Ultimate Triathlon, in which he'd rowed the Atlantic alone, climbed Mount Everest and cycled around the world. The podcast should have been fun, but while I was mission-planning it I realized I was unfamiliar with some of the challenges associated with interviewing people in front of an audience.

In the end, I leaned in to the same tactics that had previously helped me in war. I performed some intel-gathering, chatting to a few mates who had presented in a similar setting and speaking to the podcast's producer about what to expect while conducting an interview in a crowded room. Once in the pub, I checked out where I would be sitting, who I would be presenting to and how best to project myself in such a busy environment.

As I became more comfortable with the operation, it helped to visualize some of the trickier challenges ahead. Nerves were inevitable at the beginning, as they were for every talk I'd given. But I also knew that it was fairly easy to settle into the rhythm of interviewing a stranger. I had a printout of questions with me, but I wanted the conversation between Megan, James and myself to feel natural so I kept them out of sight with the intention of only using them if the talking dried up. In a way, this was the Ground section of a mission plan – *an insight into the area we were moving into and the buildings or terrain we were likely to encounter.*

I then focused on the Situation – *detail on the enemy forces in the area, the assets at their disposal and the kind of resistance we could expect to face.* There was a live audience. Would I get heckled if I messed up? Could I hold their attention? To put myself at ease, I remembered the faces staring back at me at the beginning of every talk: after a while they usually transformed into an unmemorable, shapeless blur. (No offence if you've attended any of my presentations.) The same would happen again. I'd be able to talk, draw some cracking stories from two very interesting interviewees, and have a good time. By acknowledging the upcoming challenges in my mission plan, I was able to work with a positive attitude, confident I'd prepared for every psychological obstacle ahead.

MISSION PLANNING
AND THE SMALLER DETAILS

Detail was everything in the Special Forces. Just the smallest snippet of information could sometimes be the difference between a mission going well and it descending into chaos. For instance, I would sometimes be tasked with meeting tribal elders or senior military figures from other countries. It was imperative that an elite operator was prepared for the environment because when two unfamiliar cultures came together in a meeting, a social faux pas or even the slightest mistake with a gesture might inflame tempers or cause upset. Prepping to avoid those potential errors helped to control emotions in events where tensions occasionally ran high.

So, I learned different languages and picked up valuable key phrases. It was important I conducted myself respectfully in both public and private spaces, so I'd take my shoes off when entering someone's home and I'd always accept food and drink if it was offered – regardless of whether it looked appetising or not, because to refuse was often regarded as an insult. And when shaking someone's hand I'd look that person in the eye, nodding and placing my free hand upon my heart.

Knowing I had the skills to control a potentially volatile atmosphere gave me extra confidence when going into sketchy environments later on in life, too. During the making of *Meet the Drug Lords: Inside the Real Narcos*, I always made sure to introduce myself in Spanish to some of the scary dudes I met. It wasn't a lot, but the gesture showed respect. To stick to my own language was very risky.

Picking up on small details around me was also vital in the thick of the action. I was forever scoping out my physical environment, gathering information for immediate use and, maybe, for future missions. When we first entered the Colombian *barrio*, I checked the roads we'd need to take if we had to leave in a hurry. Everybody seemed to be very jumpy; the hairs on the back of my neck were standing up. Once we'd been instructed to wait inside the shack, as the sun went down, I immediately figured out our best escape routes as a precaution. I'd decided that if a gang attacked our position while we were outside, the smart move was to dive past the shack and into the river below. If we were bumped while waiting inside, there was a window I knew we'd be able to leap from, leaving us to swim away under the cover of darkness. The water was grim, polluted and brown with sewage, which made it an excellent escape option: nobody was going to follow us through the stink. The downside was that we'd probably get really sick in the aftermath, but it was a better option than being taken hostage by a Colombian drug cartel and then tortured or murdered. Taking a second to assess the small details of my environment – and, in this case, the potential escape routes – brought a little reassurance.

MISSION-PLAN THE FINISH LINE

During mission-planning sessions, the intelligence we receive can sometimes be intimidating or troubling. Sometimes, the preparation we had to do in the run-up to a military tour or mission could be physically challenging or psychologically taxing. Instilling positive thought was an important facet of every planning process, and the military often concluded a meeting or training session with a 'look forward' so that the hard work ended on an uplifting note. We might have spent the day working on battle tactics or running as a squadron through the mud and pissing rain – screwing up and succeeding in equal measure. At the very end, a debriefing session impressed on us the important takeaway points. Once the inevitable bollockings and hard lessons were delivered, whichever senior figure was taking the course made sure to end on a positive note. For example: 'As a look forward, you can expect to be working in this way on a forthcoming operation . . .' Ending on a high was important, even if the work preceding it had been a bloody disaster.

The information gathered on the eve of my trip to Afghanistan for the filming of *Foxy's War* made for grim reading. In the run-up to the job, Channel Four had brought in a company called Secret Compass, an organization that assessed safety issues for TV filming locations. On a scale of one to ten for danger, my trip was very much at the higher end. Kabul was chaos. Suicide bombers were striking every day and there were reports of armed attacks. A lot of people were getting killed. When I'd been in the Special Forces, our procedures and personnel had given me a fair level of reassurance; as a civilian, negotiating the unsettling picture of what was happening on the ground in Afghanistan felt a little trickier.

Luckily I'd found a new and effective technique for managing any troublesome intelligence in the mission-planning process. During my recovery from PTSD, I'd worked with Malcolm Williams, a therapist experienced in treating military veterans suffering from similar issues to mine. While chatting to Malcolm at Rock2Recovery, I picked up several processes for managing anxiety and stress during missions. One such technique involved the visualization of successful outcomes to challenging situations. Malcolm first mentioned this a week before a high-profile event where I was due to give a talk. At the time, appearing in public was a new thing for me. I wasn't well versed in making speeches or delivering presentations to big crowds. Just the thought of doing so put me into a bit of a spin, so I turned to Malcolm for advice.

'Don't worry,' he said, having listened to my concerns. 'Let me give you a three-step exercise.'

Malcolm then asked me to think about the talk and how I'd feel once it had been delivered perfectly.

'Imagine those ten seconds after your talk has finished,' he said. 'Everything's gone great and you're feeling fantastic, elated. Now focus on that sensation, the emotions. Close your eyes and for fifteen minutes think about those ten seconds, the exhilarating sensation of success, and nothing else.'

The next phase of the exercise, explained Malcolm, would take place a couple of hours later. 'Picture the scene at home on the day of the talk, after everything is done,' he said. 'You're talking about the presentation to your wife, explaining to her how it went. Yeah, you might remember a few stutters, a couple of anecdotes that might have gone better, but overall you're still excited about how it went. Imagine that sensation and how it makes you feel.'

The final stage of the exercise was set to take place right before bedtime. Once again I had to visualize a moment of satisfaction, as I'd done for steps one and two. This time I was settling down to sleep feeling happy about the presentation, proud of my work.

'You're buzzing about the talk and probably wondering what you were worried about in the first place,' explained Malcolm, before telling me to repeat the process every day until the event was over. Over the following week, I told myself to live in the afterglow of success, where any stresses about the highly pressurized presentation had been forgotten. As a result, I was able to see past my nervousness; by focusing on the buzz of a successful talk, the anxieties I'd been experiencing faded away. Eventually I felt so relaxed about what I had to do that the event became a breeze – I nailed every point I'd wanted to get across.

I've since applied that technique to many stressful situations, including my return to Afghanistan. Rather than dwelling on the scarier elements of my mission plan, I visualized myself relaxing on the long flight home, experiencing all the positive emotions after a successful work trip. *You're sitting in the plane, sipping on a beer, staring at the chaos of Afghanistan below. You're feeling chuffed with the work you've finished. The crew have grabbed some great footage and a series of brilliant interviews. You know exactly how you want the documentary to look and feel, and everyone at Channel Four is going to be chuffed.*

I wasn't living in denial; I understood the risks of returning to Afghanistan and I knew that vigilance would be imperative once I was on the ground. (From the minute we landed, our car was trailed by a gang of armed men on scooters. Our driver was able to lose them with a series of smart manoeuvres.) But when the work began for real, it helped to imagine the time straight after the mission, when the hard yards were done and I was safely en route home. It kept my focus away from any fear so that I only had to concentrate upon the job in hand.

OPERATIONAL DEBRIEF

» Mission planning is everything. Use all the intelligence at your disposal to build a picture of the tests ahead. With intel you can construct a 360-degree image of your challenge and prepare for the obstacles accordingly.

» For potentially emotionally charged situations, battle-prep the mind with intel on where you're going, what you're doing and what to expect when you get there. If you can, bring an experienced head with you to help.

» Picture yourself at the finishing line. Imagine you've nailed a high-pressure presentation; you've smashed your first 10K run; a month has passed since you've puffed on a ciggy. Feel the buzz of success and the sense of achievement. Now use those emotions to get you there for real.

SITUATIONAL AWARENESS

PAUSE FOR BREATH

In the immediate aftermath of an event or action where a reactionary strike might take place, a troop of soldiers often immersed themselves in a 'Soak Period' – a chunk of time where it seemed prudent to wait in order to see if their presence had been detected. I often did this during ambush situations when my unit crept through a series of rendezvous (RV) points under the cover of darkness before taking up a position where we could attack the enemy. After every RV the group fanned out into a defensive position and halted, often for half an hour.

The routine was often a little hairy. When moving through undergrowth, it was sometimes hard to work silently, especially as a body of men. Leaves rustled, branches snapped. Even just taking off a bergen rucksack could cause a disturbance. To ensure we hadn't been spotted or heard while moving into a vulnerable position, it was vital to remain still in the minutes immediately after we'd settled; moving on to the next RV too quickly might see the enemy opening fire on us.

The assessment period wasn't 100 per cent guaranteed – everything was delivered on instinct, and decisions were made based on how close we were to the enemy, what the terrain looked like ahead and where we were on the ground. However, a lot can be taken away from the military Soak Period, and each of us can apply it to our resilient lives, usually after a big decision or event has taken place. For example:

1) The athletic individual recovering from an illness or injury shouldn't jump right back into their normal routine because the kickbacks could be debilitating. Instead, they should embark on a session of light training, before settling into a Soak Period to ensure they don't have any negative reactions.

2) When buying equipment from a new, potentially regular supplier, a company should first purchase a smaller shipment to assess the process, quality and overall relationship before committing to a larger order.

Pressing on quickly with the next training session or contract without thought or care leaves us vulnerable to a nasty surprise. But the Soak Period enables us to deal with any negative responses to our actions, should they be waiting to strike.

PHASE NINE

DEVELOPING EMOTIONAL CONTROL

Even the most resilient of us can become emotionally overwhelmed in situations where mental grit is required.

For example, much of our forward momentum can be undone by fear: the fear of failure; the fear of success; the fear of criticism; the fear of pain. Some of us are dominated by smaller but no less impactful phobias, such as flying or enclosed spaces. But if we're to become resilient, it helps to overcome any psychological hurdles of this nature, or at least to manage them in such a way that they're unable to halt our progress.

This is a truth I've learned the hard way. Once I'd started to engage in combat as part of the British military, my sense of my mortality was tested on a daily basis. Every day there was a chance I might die, and at times it was difficult to manage the anxiety. Handily, I quickly discovered several techniques that helped to compartmentalize my stresses – but only if I acknowledged them in the first place and then worked to manage their impact. With time, I was able to apply the same methods to all kinds of negative emotions.

Not everybody's the same, especially in civilian life. I've noticed that people can act irrationally when experiencing psychological pressure. In scary situations, some individuals become angry or overwhelmed, and their fear results in their downfall, whatever that might be. Others feel embarrassed when experiencing grief, and lash out or became withdrawn. With a little know-how, however, it's possible that such individuals could manage their negative emotions and turn them into a positive force.

I want to start this chapter by detailing an emotional low point, a moment when stress threatened to overwhelm me.

The hard arrest was in chaos. One of our lads had been horrifically wounded and the image of his shooting stuck in my mind for hours after we'd cleared the building, taken down his killer and swept the rooms for intel and weapons. For the first time in my military career, I'd actually feared for my life. *PTSD was setting in.* This might sound stupid, but up until that moment I'd never considered the fact that I might die while operating for the British Armed Forces. I'd trusted my training to keep me safe. For years I'd been swaddled in a bubble of ignorance, unaware of the mortal risks facing me, or perhaps subconsciously unwilling to accept them. *Talk about stupid.* It had taken me twenty years to realize I was working in a bloody dangerous job.

Night was falling. I crouched behind a wall, surveying the wreckage from our operation. There were several dead people around us, all enemy fighters, but the area wasn't secured and we were holding our position in a maze-like compound, awaiting our next instructions. From my location I could see a courtyard and several doors, each one leading into alleyways that felt more like rabbit warrens – whenever I'd been forced into one it had been impossible not to feel disorientated, there were so many blind corners and dead ends. I looked up. From a ladder above me, one of our lads, a trained sniper, was watching out for incoming hostiles. All of us sensed that we might get bumped at any moment. I dreaded the idea. *I was worried.*

I don't want to get up from behind this wall, I thought.

Up until that moment I'd been fairly fearless on operations, but pragmatic, too. I wasn't one to run around like a headless chicken, but I threw myself into the work, 100 per cent. Suddenly, my role as an operator felt like an effort. *It was emotional.* And when the call eventually came for me to clear another series of rooms, my heart raced when ordinarily it would have been calm and steady. I stood up and ran towards the target, my body hunched over as if I'd been punched in the gut, in what was a desperate attempt to make myself smaller.

I was terrified. Functional, but terrified all the same. I racked my brains for any excuse not to go into the next building. *Can't someone else do it? Maybe I could twist my ankle on the run over and send another lad in my place?* But an opportunity to pass on the responsibility wasn't going to present itself. The door was kicked in and we moved through the building, our weapons up, only to find ourselves in a family home, abandoned apart from some old furniture. I puffed out a sigh of relief, but my mind still raced. I wanted to get out of harm's way. And then the comms in my ear crackled. It was my Officer Commanding.

'Right, we want you to walk on to a location that's around a kilometre-and-a-half away from here,' he said. 'It's another compound we'd like you to check over.'

My heart sank. *For fuck's sake.* I'd hoped to get out of there sharpish, back to base for a wet and some downtime, but instead we had to creep through a field of head-high poppies, my senses alert to any people who may or may not have been moving around us, waiting to open fire. I found myself visualizing the moment where I came face to face with a gunman. As far as I was concerned, work was bound to get noisy again at any moment . . .

Or maybe not. Having finally arrived at our target, we kicked through the place in double-quick time. Beyond the first door was a herd of goats. Panicked by our entrance, they crowded around us, bleating and jumping this way and that in a right tizz. The second door led us into an old barn with a population of two: one shitting cow and a farmer who looked fairly annoyed, having realized his goats were now running wild outside.

I was just as moody. Night had come and it was freezing cold. My unit was now faced with a three-kilometre trek back to our landing zone, a man down. It was hard not to feel demoralized after spending an hour nervously anticipating my impending death, only to assault a barn of livestock. *What was the point in that?* I couldn't control my thinking. My emotions seemed to be running away with me during an operation, which I knew to be a dangerous sign for someone in my line of work. My mental health had become frazzled and, as a result, some of the techniques I'd learned for controlling my negative thoughts had been forgotten. I needed to reset.

MANAGING OUR FEARS

Superhumanity. It's a term I've sometimes used to describe the feeling of operating in the British military elite, but it's a little tongue-in-cheek. During my time in combat, all of us involved carried a weakness or two, small cracks in our armour that caused us to worry or to overthink a situation. What elevated us above other wings of the British Armed Forces was that we made a point of honing in on those weaknesses, ruthlessly and effectively, managing them in such a way that they wouldn't distract us from our mission, no matter what type of job we were on or how hairy it got.

For example, I didn't particularly like swimming in the sea. I still don't, and that might be considered pretty weird given that I served with the Royal Marines and Special Forces for twenty years. During military service I simply shut out that particular anxiety by telling myself that it would only stand in the way of my doing the job I loved. But if ever I get in the water now I'm fine-tuned to the dangers. I get a little uncomfortable and imagine sharks darting about beneath me, sizing up their next feed. Whenever I go on holiday and someone says, 'Fancy a dip?' I'll always get in, but I'm very aware of the risks.

Emotionally, I was often scared of failure during my time in the military; I didn't want people to think I couldn't handle my job. It stressed me out at times during Selection and my biggest mistake when passing out was to believe that all the hard work was over with. The reality was very different. I was thrown into an environment where responsibility was dumped upon me almost immediately; the training felt relentless, too, and I seemed to lurch out of my comfort zone with everything we did. I abseiled out of helicopters and fast-roped down buildings. I climbed on to mocked-up enemy ships and kicked in doors on pretend raids. It was the all-action stuff I'd imagined doing when I first signed up for Selection. But every now and then I'd wobble a little bit, worried that I was fucking up in a big way, when in reality I was coping pretty well.

My biggest problem, though, was my discomfort when operating at heights – I became a little nervous whenever I was abseiling down the face of a dam or out of a helicopter. As a kid, I can remember the phobia threatening to reduce me to tears. I was eight or nine years old, on a school trip, and I'd been offered the chance to abseil down a small cliff with some mates. I peered over the edge. It probably wasn't that much of a drop, but it felt like Mount Everest to me. My bottom lip trembled.

'It's OK, Jason,' said the instructor, noticing the building waterworks. 'You can walk away if you don't want to do it.'

But I didn't want to walk away because to do so made me feel like a failure. There was a pause. The drop below was far scarier than anything I'd seen before at the time and in the end I caved in to my apprehension.

No way, I thought. *I'm not going down there.*

That fear has stuck with me ever since, but I have no idea where it started. Mum hadn't warned me away from heights when I was little. However, my dad had often taken my brother and me on holiday to Cornwall, and though he always liked us to roam free, if ever we were running close to a cliff edge he'd always tied a rope around us, with the other end attached to his waist. I'd often think, *Why am I being held to this?* It wasn't that Dad was being an overly cautious or nervous parent. He was mainly making sure we were being safe at all times, but perhaps his tactic impacted upon me in a negative way, like some childhood experiences do. I never really got over it. Today, when I'm working up high, I often feel a shiver of adrenaline and get a little edgy.

I see that happen in a lot of kids now. Most of our phobias arrive with experience. If you don't believe me, compare the reaction of toddlers and adults in a pub garden at the end of summer. When a wasp inevitably arrives, the grown-ups tend to flap at the table; they freak out at anything buzzing around them. But the toddlers don't care. They'll happily allow a wasp to land in their buggy, unaware of the sting they might receive if they grab at it. Once they're a bit older, those kids will probably share the same fear as their parents, either because they've been stung or because they've watched Mum and Dad acting irrationally every time they've opened a bottle of wine in wasp weather.

But those phobias – water, heights, wasps, and the fear of failure – can be managed, as most demons can.

Yes, it takes some serious work. Having trained in the jungle, for example, I understood that recognizing my fears was another step in the self-awareness process (as detailed in Phase Seven). I hated the bugs in there, they were a nightmare, but I used the three rules of basic psychological admin to overcome any associated stress. Firstly, I accepted my dislike of insects and I decided the related stress was rational because scorpion stings bloody hurt. I then used that fear to sharpen my resolve. Finally, I focused on changing my mindset and figured, *Well, I can either spend a shitload of time running around and freaking out at every spider here, or I can sort my shit out.*

Through persistence, I was also able to overcome my nervousness around heights. I had to because there was no hiding from my anxieties. One of the many specialist courses I completed was jump training, where I parachuted out of planes day after day. On the first morning, my nerves jangled and I was pretty quiet with the other lads as they joked around and readied their kit. Wanting to tackle my problem head-on, I'd decided that listening to some of the other operators around me – the ones claiming they couldn't have cared less about the work ahead – wasn't helping in any way. Instead, I thought about how hard I'd already worked and about the adventures ahead. Did I really want a fear of heights to stop me from doing a job I loved?

Not a chance.

I focused and reset my thinking. Rather than crumbling under the pressure, I turned my nervousness on its head by looking beyond the jumps. I saw the bigger rewards and told myself that overcoming my phobia was a means to an end. I was finally doing my dream job in the military. By digging deep and applying the idea of making small steps towards success, I took each jump as a self-contained event, rather than picturing seven days of nerve-shredding leaps from a plane. Immediately, the challenge seemed so much more manageable. Jump by jump, I became a little more impervious to the fear; the doubting chitchat in my head quietened a little. And every time I experienced a minor wobble, I reminded myself of my purpose and stepped out confidently. The surge of adrenaline every time my feet hit the ground was incredible.

A highlight of my training schedule was a course nicknamed the 'Pepsi Max Week', a series of insertion techniques that wouldn't have looked out of place in a *Mission: Impossible* film or a soft-drink commercial. I jumped out of planes, set off explosives and rode in speeding boats. I then pushed myself even further. To improve my confidence with heights, I went on holiday with a mate in San Diego, where we spent a lot of time skydiving. For several days the pair of us got up early and drove to the nearby naval base, where we trained on camp, even though we were on leave, before doing jumps at 15,000 feet.

At first it was beautiful. I saw the Tijuana Mountains, and if I turned myself around, mid-air, it was possible to make out downtown San Diego and the Pacific Ocean, but after a number of jumps I realized two things: 1) For me, being in the military had ruined a lot of the events some people (not me) might consider fun, like parachuting or diving, because after a while the adrenaline rush wasn't there any more (but that was good because the fear wasn't as intense, either) and 2) *I was on bloody holiday.* And so I spent the next week of our break on the piss, confident that when it came to heights, knowledge, or in this case the experience of repeated parachute jumps, had dispelled any nerves I might have had – for a while, at least.

Fear management is a useful tool and any resilient individual should be able to recognize their anxieties and work with them. In a business setting, it might be that a team leader hates negotiating deals but their position requires them to haggle with a client over a new contract. Events like this can strike fear into a person. Luckily, there are tactics to cope, using the negotiating process as an example:

1) Switch on: use the pressure as focus; concentrate the mind on those smaller practices that will affect the bigger picture, such as your body language, or maintaining a steady and calm breath.

2) Practice: take on your own version of jump training. Build up to the Big Event by closing smaller deals with less influential clients.

3) Remember your purpose: do you really want your nervousness to stand in the way of your career or future goals?

4) If the worst comes to the worst: delegate the task to a senior member of staff who feels more comfortable when negotiating under pressure. It might feel like a cop-out, but one of the core values of leadership is the understanding of one's strengths and weaknesses. In an operational setting, the military often uses a similar technique. The team leader controls the mission and delegates the point man to go in first; the comms guy to focus on the radio; the medic to patch up the injured. Square pegs go into square holes and if even the most senior figure isn't suitable for a specialized job, it gets passed on to the relevant operator. If you're unsure whether you're the right person to debate the deal, encourage your team to complete the brutal assessment exercise detailed in Phase Seven.

THE POWER OF PATIENCE

In grim situations, it's common to watch individuals rushing towards their own death without thinking. The natural emotional response is to move quickly to get to the finishing line so that the pain, whatever that might be, can come to an end. But in war, patience is everything. To panic or to act hastily can be a self-destructive action, and on *SAS: Who Dares Wins* I've watched many people fall victim to their own rash thinking when forced into an uncomfortable position. Rather than sucking in a settling breath and taking some time to consider their next move, they allow pain, stress or fatigue to overcome them. Then they make a rash move.

One example of this was Kim Ngo on Series Five. Kim was strong, mentally and physically, despite her diminutive size, and she'd shown resilience all the way through to the final four. Having negotiated the 'Interrogation Phase', the group was then shoved through another day of endurance tests, which was where Kim broke down. She was exhausted. Lasting the course seemed beyond her, even though she was giving it her best shot. Sadly, she lost concentration for a couple of minutes when the recruits were taken to a lake and ordered to submerge in a drown-proofing test, as mentioned in Phase Five. She was unable to control her movements and breathing in the strong undercurrents and couldn't drop to the bottom as instructed.

The lake was freezing and Kim admitted to us as she stepped in that she wasn't a strong swimmer. The water swallowed her up;

in her moment of weakness, she was unable to finish the task and we had to take her armband away. It was a shame. A lot of the lads were secretly willing her on to the end. But had she taken a moment to think, there's a chance she could have progressed.

Patience and rational thought were instilled in me from the minute I joined the Royal Marines. Their importance was later amplified in the military elite because corner-cutting and rushed action were often detrimental to a mission. Nowhere was this more evident than in ambush training, where operators were ordered to wait for hours on end until a target walked into their trap, to then be shot at. My first experience of ambush training took place in the jungle and it was horrific: hot and extremely humid, our location was a disgusting area of undergrowth inhabited by all manner of creepy-crawlies. Bugs slithered and crawled over me for twelve hours, but I couldn't shift my position or shake them off me because it might alert our mock enemy if they were moving nearby.

Caution was everything. As everybody moved into position, the commander would announce over the comms that the ambush was set. At once, all the operators involved turned off the safety catches on their weapons. (For the group to do it at a later moment, when the targets might be walking past, ran the risk of alerting those hostile forces to our presence.) With most ambushes there were usually men placed in two early-warning positions, or 'cut-offs', on the left- and right-hand side of the waiting operators. It was their job to alert the rest of the group to any approaching target, and they did so by tugging at a cord that was attached to every individual's finger within the killer group. (Sometimes it was quite easy to fall asleep, and before you knew it

your finger was being yanked as everyone else moved into action.)
Once our targets had stepped into a suitable position, it was the
killer group's role to let rip; when the shooting stopped, the operators working as cut-offs then became a search party, checking
the 'dead' mock enemy for ammo, weapons and intelligence.

A lot of patience and discipline was required for a successful
ambush set-up, as it was for so many aspects of jungle training.
Everything moved slowly. Our movements were usually restricted
by the vegetation around us (as I've mentioned before, to wriggle
quickly out of the razor-sharp grip of a Bastard Tree could result
in some nasty injuries), navigation was hard and ambush actions
involved a mega-long set of orders that could be quite easy to
screw up if you rushed through them. Elsewhere, war involved
long periods of waiting around which were interspersed by
flashpoints of hardcore violence. Observation posts could be
mind-numbingly dull, too: two or three weeks of hiding out,
with our eyes trained on an enemy outpost or a suspected terrorist base, was a grind. Meanwhile, the comings and goings of
people and vehicles had to be logged meticulously. To skip a few
details or take your eye off the ball might result in some valuable
intel slipping by, and the consequences of that were sometimes
disastrous. Observation posts were uncomfortable and boring,
but patience and precision were imperative.

How this work translates to real life is really quite interesting.
At certain times, all of us are exposed to long, drawn-out episodes of negative emotion: sadness, anxiety, grief, shame, fear
and stress are all examples of discomfort that can cause us to
struggle. But often, rushing through those periods in an attempt
to get past them can cause greater problems down the line.

People numb their pain with alcohol; they pretend they're OK when really they're not; and they ignore the warning signs telling them that they're steering into trouble. Grief is an excellent example because people handle it in so many different ways. Some bottle it up, ignoring the pain until it festers, becoming a traumatic, emotional cancer; others shut out the hurt with booze, drugs or some other vice; or anger becomes the release. But I've learned that, outside of war, the only way to deal with grief healthily is to accept its value as a healing process and work through it with time and understanding.

In war it was a different story. I had to temporarily shut out pain in order to do the job I needed to do. But when I was at home, I gave my emotions the respect and the time they deserved – dealing with negative feelings can be a protracted process and it takes patience to work through it thoroughly. That allowed me to manage myself effectively; being honest and patient about what I was feeling prevented me from reacting in a way that could have been negative. So far, I've not had to deal with too many familial losses. Thankfully, both my parents are still around, but I've lost grandparents and, while I was pained by their deaths, I was always truthful about how I was feeling in the moment. That meant I could bounce back relatively quickly. When friends died during war, I often felt sad once I'd returned home. I'd grieve and there were moments when I cried for people, but I was always fairly robust. Handling my emotions with respect and due process allowed me to function. The same went for fear, stress, anxiety and all manner of negative emotions. Patience and considered thought were the only ways to manage those stressful episodes effectively.

OPERATIONAL DEBRIEF

》 Unlearn your fears. Take an honest look at what frightens you most and work towards overcoming those anxieties. Remember: *knowledge dispels fear.* A tactical approach to dealing with a phobia is to use the step-by-step mentality. For example, the team leader with a dislike of negotiating can move forward in increments by first taking on small contractual discussions before building up to that career-defining boardroom deal.

》 Patience is everything in war. Don't rush to your own death during uncomfortable situations by trying to force through a negative emotion or situation too quickly. Instead, acknowledge the discomfort, give it the respect it deserves and manage your way through the pain accordingly. Quick fixes rarely work when the stakes are high.

》 Remember your *why*. Don't let a phobia or hang-up stand in the way of your long-term goals.

SITUATIONAL AWARENESS

SLOWING LIFE DOWN:
THE CIGAR MOMENT

There are some terrifying moments that can't be prepared for. No amount of training can ready you for an unexpected accident, such as a car crash, or for a personal disaster – perhaps serious illness hits out of nowhere (did anyone see the Covid-19 crisis coming?). Incidents like these, along with freak financial events, unexpected outbreaks of violence or injuries to loved ones, can cause us to spin out emotionally.

Those moments were all too frequent in war, when even the basic procedure of commuting to work could be fraught with mortal risk. During one operation, I was part of a squadron flying out to a Tactical Landing Zone (TLZ) from where we were expected to launch a series of missions, but even the very basic step of getting to the TLZ nearly killed us. Our method of transport was a Hercules Mk 5 plane and the pilot was an individual who was known to be pretty cocksure. As we came in to land, I noticed the TLZ was so makeshift that the area hadn't been marked out in any way. We were being guided in by a couple of blokes waving their arms about on the ground. And that's when the trouble started.

Our pilot, for no apparent reason, decided to bank sharply as we descended – too sharply. I looked out of the window and crapped myself when I noticed how close to the ground we were. It seemed as if the wingtips were about to hit the dirt. Everybody started shouting and yelling angrily. *Mate, what the fuck are you doing?* When the plane straightened out seconds later, we were only metres above the so-called runway, and the wheels touched down with a loud bang. The plane pitched upwards and everybody on board seemed to become weightless for a split second before we bounced off the desert floor several times. The group was unnerved; having come to a stop, a lot of the lads went looking for the pilot, hoping to bang him out. We'd nearly been killed before the fighting had even kicked off.

I sat by the plane afterwards, rattled by what had happened. A lot of people would have gone into shock, having been nearly ended in a crash, but I leaned on a technique that had always settled my nervous system during a gunfight. I sucked in a deep, settling breath then puffed the air out slowly. I then repeated the process again in an act sometimes referred to as the 'Cigar Moment'.

The Cigar Moment was named after the famous Hamlet Cigars television adverts from the 1980s, in which a hapless individual would screw up in embarrassing fashion before calming themselves down by sparking up a cigar. They'd take in a deep draw of tobacco and then slowly blow away a plume of smoke. It was a calming moment, the inference being that everything was going to be cool, regardless of whatever disaster had just occurred.

Despite the jokey name, the Cigar Moment technique was rooted in physiology. By taking two deep, slow breaths, the body is able to turn on the vagus nerve – a cranial nerve – which controls the body's response to stress, relaxing the body and slowing the heart rate. This one action enabled an individual to calm down sufficiently before rationalizing what had happened, or was still happening. From there they could decide upon their plan of action and react accordingly. Those moments were important when looking to settle myself and I'd then crack on with whatever it was I had to do. Under the wing of our Hercules, I was able to focus on the mission ahead.

Don't rush into your own death. It's an idea I've put to a lot of people whenever they ask my advice on how to stay calm during stressful situations. In short: give yourself some room to breathe. An event might be full of emotion, but everybody is in a position to control their reactions to it. Take a home-buying scenario, for example. It might be that an individual is being asked to sign an important document with far-reaching implications for their financial security. If that person feels a little unsure, it's a smart play to slow down the moment and take two settling breaths before acting positively. If the situation still feels unsettling, it's a suitable point to hold fire and check that all the angles have been covered. The individual can say, 'Wait, let me go through this again because something doesn't feel right . . .'

When resilience is called for, the Cigar Moment delivers the right amount of breathing room, especially when time might be in short supply. And if it can work in a gunfight or a near-miss plane crash, it can work just about anywhere.

PHASE TEN

WHEN THE BATTLE'S DONE

No matter the challenges facing us, it's easy to imagine we'll emerge only as winners or losers, with nothing in between; the event will either overwhelm us or strengthen our self-belief. But as in war, life isn't defined solely in black and white, and the boundaries between victory and defeat can sometimes be blurred. Sure, our successes have the potential to embolden us, but they can cause us problems down the line, too. Meanwhile, all our failures have the potential to be transformative; after a period of reflection, they can turn us into forces to be reckoned with.

As a football fan, I see it all the time. Liverpool and Manchester City were the top two teams in the country for a couple of years. In 2018–19 City won the title but, weirdly, Liverpool's defining moment seemed to happen after they'd finished second that same year. Though they won the Champions League, losing out to Manchester City gave them the fire to push harder the following season. Meanwhile, City, having won the Premier League, then seemed to fall short during the next campaign. Liverpool were by far the better team and finished top of the table.

In the military, it's easy to fall into those same traps. After a tactical victory or a successful raid, it is a very human reaction to relax. But, unlike football, there are no pre-season or half-time breaks in war and all operators have to remain constantly alert. Meanwhile, following a defeat, it's natural to feel overwhelmed or disheartened but, as Liverpool proved, if a team or individual can draw lessons from their failures it's possible to bounce back stronger than ever before.

MAXIMIZE THE WINS, MINIMIZE THE LOSSES

There was no room to rest in the immediate hours after an operation or gunfight. It was during that time that an operator's recall was at its strongest and every step of what had happened during a mission – good and bad – could be detailed with clarity. As soon as we'd stepped off a chopper or walked on to the base, my squadron would be called into a debrief meeting in order to run over our successes and failures; it was a learning process. I've run through the finer details of a gun battle in some pretty strange places: dried-out riverbeds in the middle of the night; aircraft hangars at the crack of dawn; I've even shivered through a debrief in an abandoned city-centre building following a counterterrorism training operation.

The locations were irrelevant. The only thing that mattered was our recollection of events and the lessons that could be drawn from our wins and losses. No detail was left out; minor intelligence sometimes proved valuable later on, where the smallest snippets of information had the potential to lead us into tactically valuable conclusions or a breakthrough. The trick, as with observation posts, was to record everything that had happened on the ground without speculation or judgement. Our squadron was then able to create a vivid picture of an operation, an enemy, or our own practices. Everybody's voice in the team was considered equal, to ensure that no detail was left out during debrief sessions.

One of the many things I loved about working as an elite military operator was the lack of hierarchy. Yes, there was a chain of authority, as there had to be in any important organization, but the traditional order of command was looser than in other sections of the military. There were senior officers running the squadrons and, within that larger group, team leaders attached to the smaller units, but generally the lads were considered to be on fairly equal terms. This was particularly important in planning sessions and debriefs. It was understood that any individual might contribute a game-changing piece of information regardless of rank and experience, and everyone was encouraged to add their observations.

Meanwhile, the overall results of our missions were irrelevant to how we approached debriefs: meetings were equally detailed for losses as they were for victories; sometimes the hardest lessons were learned during a successful job rather than one that had been executed poorly. I was involved in a number of tactically effective operations that then fell apart because a unit had taken their foot off the pedal during the buzz of victory. Their overconfidence led to chaos. Rather than letting defeated hostiles flee the scene, operators gave chase and were injured as a result. Door Kickers smashed through an extra compound to grab more ammo or prisoners, only to face violent resistance that pushed them back. At times, those decisions led to unnecessary casualties within the squadron, which then impacted the group later on in the tour. Injured operators were useless assets but were rarely replaced with incoming support. Without their assistance our workload increased, and that was particularly challenging on tours where missions took place on a nightly basis. In the debriefs afterwards it was usually stated clearly that any acts of over confidence shouldn't be repeated.

Lesson-learning was equally valuable on botched jobs, or operations where events beyond our control had overtaken us. Sometimes we were overwhelmed by a burst of unexpected resistance when landing on an enemy target; our intelligence had been a little off and a larger enemy force had arrived to defend the location. In those cases we made sure to withdraw quickly, preserving our resources for a later date rather than rushing into battle, but we would always make the most of our predicament. Observations would be made on how the enemy had set up their defence systems; we'd take note of the type of weaponry they were using and how it was being utilized around their position. Were they aggressive or defensive? Did they tend to retreat under a prolonged show of force? The process was referred to as a Sensitive Site Exploitation, or SSE. Sometimes deliberately poking the hornets' nest to watch their reaction was a smart tactic.

An SSE was also a useful process to employ if a target had moved away from their reported location. Every now and then we'd receive intel that a person of interest had taken up position in a certain town or compound. Having been given the orders to swoop in to make a hard arrest, we'd kick in a few doors only to discover that the target had moved on. Our intel might have been out of date, or plain wrong, but often high-level hostiles moved from location to location in order to avoid exactly that type of capture. However, whenever our plans were upended, we didn't sulk, and we'd never return to base with our tails between our legs. Each unsuccessful job was an opportunity to learn, an opportunity to refine our skills and tactics. We could review any gathered intelligence and work on being more effective next time.

The overall debrief process was very clinical: we only dealt in facts. It didn't matter if one of the lads had been killed on the job, for example. Or if we'd rescued a hostage whose capture was being reported all over the world, or taken out an internationally notorious terrorist figure. The size of the victory, or any losses we might have experienced, was irrelevant. Instead, we covered off the mission step by step, with as much factual detail as possible, without speculation, recalling what had taken place and what we'd seen. Maps and aerial intelligence were used to illustrate the results of a mission in a three-step process:

Step One: The Officer Commanding described the mission as he'd seen it unfolding.

Step Two: The Sergeant Major then did the same, before drawing information from the units on the ground.

Step Three: The team leaders from each unit detailed the events as they'd experienced them. *We went into the room we were assigned. We killed three enemy fighters in there* ... Any other information was irrelevant. We only focused on the task at hand and dissected our actions to learn, improve and become better.

Once a team leader had finished recounting the mission from his perspective, the remainder of each unit was then called upon to add any details that might have been missed. Often, in the chaos of a battle it was easy to lose sight of the smaller events, but once everything had been put together we were able to build a detailed, 360-degree picture of what had taken place. Throughout, we noted the areas where improvement was a necessity. We checked the practices that had worked effectively under the circumstances and took into account *Any Other Bollocks* that might require assessment.

This process was painstaking, time-consuming and exhausting, but overall these debriefs were considered an invaluable resource when making us a more resilient military asset. Once the meeting concluded, a squadron clerk was tasked with typing up the relevant intelligence and the document was then distributed to any parties in need of the information. Valuable intelligence was shared with our allies, so everybody involved in a military situation could learn from our mistakes and tactical gains. That information was also fed into the British military's training schedule, if necessary. (Such as an enemy force implementing unexpected tactical approaches when defending their compounds.) New squadrons rotating into the conflict were trained up in managing techniques and procedures based on what we'd learned; old practices were phased out if they'd become outdated or irrelevant.

Every scrap of information gathered was analysed in order to help us adapt and improve against a highly motivated and dangerous enemy who were as obsessed with evolving as we were. The forces we were scrapping against were forever watching how the British military operated in order to get a better handle on how to expose us.

It's not only the competing sides in a war that can use these processes to increase their resilience, however. The debrief process used by the military elite is applicable to any setting where a team or individual requires mental and physical grit. Consider the following examples:

#1 Midway through running the London Marathon, you experience a series of excruciating cramps that puts you out of the race. Rather than walking off the course in a strop, work through an SSE-style assessment. *How many miles did you manage before failure? Could the pain have been run off, or was it definitely a race-ender? Detail what you ate before and during the race. You should also note the stretches and preparation exercises during your build-up and list which areas of the body were affected by cramping before checking in with a physiotherapist or trainer as soon as possible afterwards.* All of this intel helps to build a bigger picture of why you crashed. More importantly, it delivers the necessary details on how you can improve next time round.

#2 Having slogged your way through a business-pitch project for a number of weeks, maybe months, you and your team are on the verge of signing a lucrative contract. Rather than sitting back and enjoying the moment, take the required precautionary steps. *Is your team still on high alert, or have they relaxed? Has every detail been squared away with your new partners? Is there anything you can do to prepare yourself for a nasty surprise or two?* (Usually, vigilance is enough to avoid those last-minute screw-ups.) Later, with the contract nailed, run through a team debrief. *Highlight the areas in which you and your colleagues performed well. Look at any examples of poor practice or close calls with failure. Then figure out how they might be avoided next time. Finally, how effective were your systems and processes? Run through the relevant working areas – communication, presentation, technology etc. – and assess whether they're still working for you.* All of this information should be collated and fed back to the team for reference during the next pitch.

#3 You seem unable to smash through your fitness goals. Maybe injuries keep holding you back. Perhaps it's hard to find the motivation required to succeed. It might be your nutrition is all over the place and you're turning into a bag of shit. Either way, failure feels inevitable and emotionally you're getting bashed up. It's time to make a change by running a debrief on your poor practices. First up, check in with your purpose. *What made you want to start this challenge in the first place?* Remind yourself of where you were on day one. Recall those days where you struggled to make it to the gym. Then run through the days where training seemed to happen easily. *What differences did you notice in your routine, preparation, diet and attitude?* Using all the intel available, build a 360-degree perspective on how you succeeded and where you failed. Work towards replicating the positive days and eliminating the negative factors holding you back.

With a little work on the small details, you'll soon notice some big improvements.

Two rules:

1) Don't rest in the aftermath of success.
2) Never ignore the lessons delivered by failure.

Learn. Then reset and go again.

THE POWER OF REST AND RESETTING

Following my final, fateful military tour in 2011, our squadron was offered the chance to fly home via Cyprus for a few days of rest and recuperation. The idea was that we could sit in the sun, smash through the beers and put our feet up in a holiday resort as a reward for our hard work. The senior officers reckoned a little resetting time abroad might help us to blow off steam before we returned home to our loved ones and the normality of domestic life. Nobody was interested. The general view was that it seemed like a waste of time.

Fuck that, I thought. *I want to get home.*

But once I'd returned home to Poole, life with my family and friends felt weird. I became detached. I couldn't get my head around the slower rhythms of life and I had too much time to pore over some of the awful stuff I'd experienced in war. Hindsight's always 20/20 but, fuck me, I wish I'd taken that holiday.

The reasoning behind the idea for a quick break had been sound. I've since learned of a somewhat infamous urban myth from the Falkland Islands after the conflict with Argentina in the early 1980s. With the war done, the British military moved their forces home. A large number of lads travelled back by boat, which took them towards ports situated in the north of England. The trip across the Atlantic lasted for a couple of weeks and, with plenty of beer on board and a reduced level of discipline, the scene turned fairly lawless. People were passing out with the booze. Brawls kicked off all over the place. But by the time Britain was in sight, everybody had exorcised a lot of their demons. The stresses of war had been worked through.

I've sometimes wondered what would have happened to me had I popped over to Cyprus instead of heading straight home. (Hopefully, I wouldn't have got myself into too many punch-ups.) A tired mind is a weakened mind, so rest and recovery was vital when preparing for emotional chaos. Working as an operator often meant I received little of either, given that I served on a succession of tours in horrible war zones for up to six months at a time. There was a break of only a few months between each tour and then I was thrust into the action again. At the time, I loved it, and I actually found life outside combat more confusing than war itself. At least in war, the rules of engagement were clear, defined in black and white, but time back in the UK was too hectic. I'd come off tour and roll straight into training, exercises and last-minute tasks. The frantic pace of life was unsustainable.

Such a frenetic schedule soon took its toll. I was doing too many tours with not enough time off in between. By the time I left the military, in 2012, I was rinsed. Burned out by a lifestyle of high stress, intense physical activity and sporadic outbreaks of controlled violence, I became detached from the people around me, depressed and suicidal. I had no way of knowing how emotionally damaged I'd become because I was rarely given enough time to reset. After war operations, I'd usually have a few hours of restless sleep before cracking on with some intelligence work for the missions ahead. In order to stay physically sharp, there were gym sessions every day; at night we'd usually get in the choppers and work on Door-Kicking raids or counterterrorism jobs. The load was exhausting.

Having come through the other side, I've learned about the importance of rest and resetting. These days, I use moments of peace and quiet to my advantage – I'll treat them as another form of admin, preparation for a period of intense physical or mental work to come. For example, if ever I'm about to speak in front of a conference room full of business people, I'll prepare quietly in a room, alone with my headphones. I'll walk about while getting my mindset right. Once the work is done, I'll enjoy some more alone time in the car, listening to the radio or a podcast. It helps to bring me down a little.

During periods of high-stress work, even the shortest moments of rest have been invaluable. While making *Meet the Drug Lords: Inside the Real Narcos* I'd often round off the day by sitting on the rooftop of our hotel, wherever we were, for a beer with my work partner, Aldo. Together we'd end up running through the events of the previous twenty-four hours, laughing at how we'd somehow managed to get through another cartel meet-and-greet without copping an assassin's bullet to the head.

Spending downtime with a mate in a safe environment helped me to reset and process everything that had happened. The routine also gave me something to look forward to when events had taken a scary turn, and I used the thought of an end-of-day bevvy as an incentive to distract me from whatever fear or stress I might have been experiencing at the time.

When readying myself for the trip, I knew that my meetings with various cartel members were going to be sketchy, but there were a number of occasions when I genuinely feared for my life. At one point, we were driven through the jungle to meet with a cocaine 'chef' – a dude producing kilos and kilos of powder from a shack in the middle of nowhere. Such was his notoriety, he wore a bandana to disguise his identity at all times, and the atmosphere was tense. En route to our meeting point, we'd been instructed to swap cars. The ride was done at night and it was imperative nobody spotted us. Had someone from the cartel noticed a car full of strangers, they were more than likely to open fire first and ask questions later, fearing we were Feds. As soon as we were dropped off, I noticed the headlights of another car approaching along the road. Our fixer for the meeting went into a panic.

'Get back into the car!' he shouted. 'They'll kill you if you're seen.'

We dived into our seats again, crouching down to avoid being spotted as the vehicle raced past. Thankfully, we were unnoticed – for now. By the time we'd wandered into the woods to meet our 'chef', tensions were running high. It was still dark, but as we filmed him working, the sun started creeping in through the trees. A feeling of nervousness arrived with it. It was obvious that we couldn't leave in daylight – we'd be easily spotted by any other narcos in the area – so we were advised to wait in a shack with those kilos of freshly batched coke and some very scary people. By mid-morning, however, our presence had been noticed by a passer-by. Word spread and soon a number of locals had gathered outside. The fixer was now very edgy.

'You have to leave now,' said the chef, anxiously.

I nodded. Quickly we gathered our kit and scarpered, a four-man team legging it through the woods, carrying random bits of camera equipment, until we'd reached the pick-up point. Thankfully another ride was waiting for us. We jumped into the back of a truck and covered ourselves with various bits of tarpaulin, clothes and bags – anything to avoid being spotted by a passing gunman. And all the way I kept my mind fixed on one simple thought.

I can't wait for that rooftop beer with Aldo.

The idea kept me sane during several terrifying hours as we drove back to the hotel.

Resetting is also vital in the wake of a positive experience. How often do we hear of couples falling into a bit of a slump in the weeks following their honeymoon? It's an understandable experience, really. For a soon-to-be-wed couple there are months, sometimes years, of planning and preparation to work through. The process is both exhilarating and exhausting. But once the wedding has happened and the party is a distant hangover, what comes next? It's easy to be overwhelmed by the normality of married life if the void isn't filled with another stimulating activity or event.

The same thing happens on expeditions to remote places. Explorers climb mountains or trek across Arctic wastelands, but once back in the safety and civility of Heathrow airport, they hit a mega-downer. Life seems mundane, the expedition bubble pops and it can take a while for the rhythm of life to feel satisfying again. The experience of moving out of war zones without an acclimatization phase has taught me that any period of healthy resetting is vital for an individual following an exhilarating life experience. Following a kayaking trip I made to the Yukon River (see Phase 12), I actively used my flight home to reset: mentally I'd registered those hours stuck in a seat on a long-haul flight as a chance to emotionally adjust. I stared out of the window and watched the epic landscape below, looking weirdly benign from thousands of metres up.

Wow, I thought. *That was an awesome expedition.*

I relived the experience in my head with a few beers, then I checked out mentally with a couple of in-flight films. By the time I'd landed, I was reset and ready to slip back into home life again. Without the manic emotions that can sometimes overwhelm a person after a life-affirming experience, I was soon back to normal speed and ready to plan my next adventure.

OPERATIONAL DEBRIEF

» During moments of defeat, or events where you might be falling short of your targets, take stock – conduct a Sensitive Site Exploitation. Note the areas in which you're not working well or breaking down, then figure out how you can improve upon them next time. It's much easier to absorb what's happening in the moment, rather than trying to remember the events and details during the days, weeks or months afterwards.

)) Always debrief after missions or challenges have been concluded, whether you've been successful or not. Improvement only happens when we're willing to assess our strengths and how to maintain them. Understanding our weaknesses and where we can improve is equally vital.

)) In team settings, remember that everyone is capable of gathering a snippet of game-changing intel, regardless of their rank or experience. Set up your system so that everyone involved can forward important notes or any ideas they might have.

)) It's important to reset after any lengthy mission or period of time where your strengths have been tested. Likewise, make sure to relax in any moments of downtime during challenging periods: don't waste mental calories that might be needed for the next battle.

)) Remember the two rules:
1) Don't rest in the aftermath of success.
2) Never ignore the frustration of failure.

SITUATIONAL AWARENESS
THE VALUE OF BOREDOM

War could be bloody boring for long periods of time. The phrase *Hurry up and wait* seemed to best illustrate what most elite military units experienced during missions. We'd race to a location or base, revved up on adrenaline, only to stand down because our target had moved or because the weather, or some other tactical factor, prevented us from attacking at the time of our choosing. Sitting around in a mess hall and killing time was an occupational hazard for many blokes trained in the art of extreme warfare, and the common complaint I'd hear from most operators was one of boredom.

'Fucking hell, I want it to kick off,' they'd say.

But a funny change in attitude usually set in once the rounds were ripping over our heads and mortar fire was exploding around us.

'Bloody hell . . . *I'm not ready!'*

For a long time I shared that mindset. But after a few tours I came to realize the importance of making the most of too much time with nothing to do. *Boredom presented me with a chance to recover for the next operation.* Having become familiar with the unpredictable schedule of combat, I learned to live in the dead hours between jobs. As soon as a sense of listlessness kicked in, I'd adjust and function in the 'now'.

Yeah, I'm bored, I'd think. *But at least I'm alive – and no one is trying to kill me.*

I used those rare moments as periods of rest, closing down my brain as best I could while conserving my energy for when life inevitably turned noisy again.

The problem with certain aspects of modern life is that we're rarely given the opportunity for boredom. As soon as our brains feel an onset of tedium, we reach for distraction: Twitter, Facebook, Instagram. These are great ways to pass the time, but they're also boredom-killers, and boredom is vital if we're to become more resilient. Boredom gives us the space to breathe, to reflect, to create and to plan. Within it, we can rest and be more effective when our energy is called upon for more important tasks. And sometimes, without boredom, we can become frazzled to such an extent that our resilience fails us.

Quite often on *SAS: Who Dares Wins* we'll come across an individual with a hectic headspace. They lead overly busy lives; due to their work, a tricky home or personal situation, or some deep-seated behavioural issue, they're unable to switch frequencies. As a result, they only know how to operate at a hundred miles per hour. Without boredom or periods of rest and reflection, they're unable to see their way through sticky situations or to problem-solve. They're constantly set to a flight-or-fight setting and their adrenal glands become shot; they buzz around the barracks or mess around with the other recruits when they could be resting or re-evaluating. When tested, they inevitably fail in ugly circumstances.

Everybody can find time to unwind and relax, mentally and physically. Put down the phone for a designated period of rest. Switch off the laptop once work is done. And dream.

Bloody hell, it's boring isn't it?

But that's the whole point.

PHASE ELEVEN

CASEVAC: COUNTING THE COST OF BATTLE

Nobody's psychologically bulletproof. Regardless of our experiences, expertise or strengths, each of us takes a hit from time to time. As I've explained, fuck-ups are an occupational hazard when striving towards resilience. But how we react to those mistakes and setbacks is what defines us. Sure, the emotional IEDs we step on will feel devastating in the moment, but that's when the 'bounce-backability', the desire to keep learning and growing, becomes so important.

Occasionally the hurdles we come up against are so big that they can't be faced alone. This is where life becomes difficult: being involved in a serious accident, experiencing a major life-change or watching a family member struggle with terminal illness might sometimes act as the detonator in a mental explosion which, if left unchecked, can wreck our lives and those of the people around us. In situations of that kind we're usually presented with a stark choice: go it alone, or put pride to one side and ask for help.

The first option might feel like the easiest path – it's certainly gentler on the ego. But I've discovered throughout my military career that acting as a lone wolf doesn't usually work, while teamwork and expert assistance are everything.

Admitting to someone that we're unable to cope is a smart move. But it's also challenging, and too many people bottle out of asking for assistance. They get scared; they're too proud to admit their shortcomings or the severity of a perilous situation they've stumbled into. But the inability to make that courageous first step can prove costly.

Operators get hurt on missions, sometimes fatally. I've been fortunate, though. During my service I managed to avoid getting taken down by a round, but some lads I knew weren't so lucky. Some mates died during gunfights; others have had their lives changed for ever by a sniper or an IED. Given the incredibly high-risk nature of our work, all elite military units included medics within their teams. These weren't civilians working in a war zone, however. Rather, they were expert operators with the capabilities to treat bullet wounds and other types of injuries someone might expect to receive in the theatre of combat. Their training focused on trauma treatment; it was their job to learn how to control any bleeding while stabilizing a patient. This gave them the basic tools to help when someone copped a round from an AK-47 or stepped on to a landmine. Life as a military medic was gnarly.

There comes a point in many military missions where one or more soldiers might become incapacitated, either physically or mentally – sometimes both. When the lives of their brothers and sisters are at risk, as in war, they might attempt to shrug aside those wounds in order to finish the mission, but that can have dangerous implications later on, for the individual and their team. There have also been countless stories of explorers losing their minds to fatigue while working through dangerous expeditions. Having approached a distant shore after months of sailing across an ocean, for example, severe exhaustion kicks in. The person's brain goes into meltdown and they make fatal decisions they would have avoided had they been at full strength. But if the explorer had radioed for assistance, they would have received the help required to complete their expedition. Likewise, had the injured soldier recognized the seriousness of their predicament and called a medic, the impact of their injury could have been minimized.

THE VALUE OF RAISING YOUR HAND

When the chips are down, most of us are too proud or too scared to ask for help. I'm not talking about the kind of assistance someone might seek out in a tricky moment, such as a bank loan during a period of limited cash flow or extra manpower when the workload becomes unexpectedly heavy. I'm talking about those events when our egos feel threatened by failure. Presented with a potential loss of face or a diminished sense of status, we ignore the safe ports in a storm. We don't call for assistance on the radio. We fail to shout out to the medic in our unit. I've heard of so many projects, lives, relationships and businesses that have fallen apart because somebody was too proud to raise their hand for assistance. The affected individual then pressed on alone, not realizing that to be patched up and CASEVACed away from a dangerous situation creates an opportunity to heal and recover before fighting again. Instead, they remain silent and bleed out.

Let's stress-test this attitude against one of the scenarios we've already mentioned in the book: the example of a failed marathon runner. Feeling frustrated at their lack of success and a little embarrassed by any inadequate preparations they might have made, the disappointed athlete thinks, *Sod asking anyone for advice. I'll crack on with another race attempt, alone.* They fail to contact a trainer or physiotherapist – someone in a position to understand exactly why their body failed during the race. The intelligence at the runner's fingertips, such as online information, running magazines and local athletics clubs, goes untapped. As a result, they lose out on a wealth of knowledge that might have helped them to avoid the mistakes of their earlier marathon attempt. Elsewhere, a potential support group of friends and family, unaware of the emotional challenges facing the athlete, isn't able to lend a helping hand.

Sometimes, though, the stakes are much higher.

It's not uncommon for people to experience a serious emotional upheaval from time to time. But how we react to it can be the difference between recovery and becoming stuck in a dangerous spiral of depression. Shame and fear leads to a weird form of emotional paralysis. Rather than seeking expert help and leaning on the people closest to them, an emotionally wounded individual battles through their predicament alone, either pretending to the outside world that they're OK – all the while internally burning – or publicly suffering a breakdown. In my case, ego wouldn't allow me to ask for expert help. I also closed myself off from friends, family and former colleagues until I became so lost that I considered killing myself. Had I called for assistance sooner, there would have been any number of friendly faces willing to help me out; a therapist or counsellor could have eased me into a healthier state of mind. But having become lost within my depression and pride, I couldn't see the escape routes.

There are many reasons why a lot of people, men especially, seem unable to ask for help when they need it most. Upbringing is partly to blame: some people are encouraged to develop a tough exterior from an early age, when they are told that emotion is a sign of weakness. But that's bollocks and fairly outdated as an idea. We all feel pain – *or at least we should when it's appropriate* – and expressing that vulnerability is a release valve. Don't misunderstand me: I'm not claiming that everyone should turn into wet lettuces at the first sign of a challenge. What I'm saying is that silence is a dangerous thing when it comes to emotional pressure. Like a wounded operator on the battlefield, to ignore the broken ankle, or to pretend that a wound isn't as serious as it really is, can be a dangerous choice. However, calling out for assistance gives an injured soldier a fighting chance at long-term success. It's the same with mental health.

Some people might claim that asking for professional help, or admitting to mates that you're in trouble, isn't a very resilient thing to do. *But is it resilient to end your life because you've been unable to see your way out of a scary or emotionally fraught situation?* Because that's the nuclear option many people consider when pressed with seemingly insurmountable problems. I've heard too many horror stories of former soldiers who started an evening with their family, eating dinner, acting like the life and soul of the party; they've then quietly excused themselves for a walk and the following day they're found dead, having decided to end it all by suicide. Often there's no explanation. The reasons for their actions go unknown and it's a tragedy.

Given my own past experience with mental health, I've attempted to emotionally bombproof my life to such an extent that hopefully I'll never again find myself standing on a cliff edge, looking down and wondering, *What would it be like to fall?* By working with expert therapists and counsellors at Rock2-Recovery, I'm able to chat through any tricky issues I might be managing before they become too much of a psychological burden. Part of my role as an ambassador for the company is to encourage clients to seek out the professional help best suited to them. For me, overall, exercise is probably the biggest key to my emotional well-being. When I'm not away filming, I like working out with a bunch of lads I respect. We get together, train hard and sometimes go for a pint afterwards. As well as being a physical commitment, those training sessions provide a pressure valve. The blokes I work out with are tough as nails – alpha males who will happily take the piss out of one another given the slightest opportunity. But between us we've created an environment where we can openly talk about some of the bad shit that's gone on in our lives, without judgement or criticism.

Not all my mates are like that. Some of the circles I move in wouldn't tolerate that kind of conversation. In those groups, expressing any emotional upset is viewed as a weakness and subject matter of that nature is dismissed pretty quickly – and that's cool. The point is this: *I have another outlet if it's needed.* It's there for when my life gets turbulent; I'm also on hand to help anyone who might be experiencing dramas of their own – with work, at home or within their family. When I'm among the group I train with, simply opening up in the right environment or listening to a mate's advice can be enough to help me course-correct emotionally.

People are generally more resilient than they think. And while no one's invincible, *everyone's brave enough to ask for help.* In times of serious trouble we should reach for the comms to contact our friends and family. When it gets really serious, everybody should understand the importance of involving a professional. Sometimes a helping hand is all it takes to get a chaotic life back on track.

UNDERSTANDING ROCK BOTTOM

All operators are taught to watch out for 'combat indicators': signs that trouble is nearby or that an enemy attack is imminent. These clues could be subtle. Piles of dirt or rubble by the side of a road or pathway might hint at the presence of a recently planted IED. An unusual lack of activity in a normally busy town could suggest the locals have been tipped off about an impending ambush. Nine times out of ten, the pile of rubble by the road is the result of a burrowing animal or a rockfall; the unusually quiet town is nothing more than a coincidence. Nevertheless, those combat indicators are always taken seriously because to ignore them is to tempt fate, and the consequences of a booby-trapped pathway or unexpected sniper attack are too horrific to ignore.

Telltale signs of this kind are also applicable to our mental resilience. Having spent a few years helping battle-broken men and women with Rock2Recovery, not to mention some of the recruits on *SAS: Who Dares Wins* whose lives had taken shocking and unimaginable twists (and led them to a point where they were strong enough to test themselves against the military's toughest selection process), I've come to know the combat indicators for mental health. It's sometimes easier to spot them in another person because the brain can become so stressed out and fatigued that it doesn't always recognize an ambush closer to home.

My own experience of mental health issues followed a common pattern: I became withdrawn, angry and fuzzy-headed. I could be very forgetful, too, to the point that, having told a friend one night that I was driving around looking for a tree to hang myself from, the following day, when that same friend called to check on my state of mind (luckily I'd been coaxed home), I couldn't remember my behaviour or the frantic conversation we'd had. (I was stone-cold sober, before you ask.) Despite those emotional warning signs, it would be a while before I sought help. For months I shrugged off people's concerns; I ignored the danger I was in because I couldn't really see it myself, and I was only fixed once a work colleague had actively nudged me in the direction of a good therapist.

Cleared of the stress from my misfiring head, I became aware of a series of signals that would have encouraged me to seek help at a much earlier stage, had I understood them. Of course, these warning signs can vary from person to person (for example, some people self-harm, others embark on dangerous booze and drug benders), but over the following pages I'll detail some of the symptoms I've become familiar with. Should a serious emotional ambush strike again, I know exactly which combat indicators to watch out for. Learning about them might assist you, too, or at least help you to spot any conflicts in those closest to you.

#1 Hyper-vigilance

A troubling symptom of intense stress, the hyper-vigilant mind is an overly busy one. Following an extreme event – a physical assault or a car crash, for example – our brains can go into self-protection functionality: we look for danger when there is none, such as in a crowded supermarket or pub. We become stressed in situations where there's nothing to worry about unduly; danger status is applied to innocuous settings and we become constantly fearful, tense and anxious. It's not uncommon for the person affected to lose their temper at the drop of a hat. In my case, the issue was intensified by my vocation. In war I'd been trained to protect myself and the lives of the lads around me. A neurological fight-or-flight programme was hardwired into my mind and it became tough to snap out of it once my service was over. I couldn't settle into a normal routine at home.

Life experiences don't have to be as harsh as the ones I endured for them to be incapacitating. Someone unfortunate enough to have been involved in a shocking event, such as an earthquake or a house fire, can be upset by loud noises and unexpected movements long after the initial incident has passed. In the aftermath, their memory can overload with a library of sights, sounds and smells associated with the original trauma. Anything that later resembles those sensory cues can be enough to kick-start an unpleasant emotional response. Some of the blokes I knew in the early phases of my career were old enough to have served in Northern Ireland. They'd been subjected to mob attacks, petrol bombs and group protests that had turned incredibly violent without warning. Having retired, some of them were affected negatively by a normal occurrence at a civilian event: a raised voice in a party, a crying baby in a pram or the sound of two shopping trolleys colliding in a supermarket were among the catalysts for responses ranging from deep depression to violence. The most innocent of happenings would emotionally transport them straight back to 1980s Belfast, working amid The Troubles.

I've also met people who have been deeply affected by an outbreak of violence in a peacetime setting. My colleague at Rock2Recovery, Malcolm Williams, was once beaten up by a mob of West Ham fans after a game against his football team, Luton Town. He was walking to the train station, minding his own business, when there was a tap on the shoulder. A voice called out to him.

'Oi, mate . . .'

When he turned around, Malcolm was smashed in the face. He dropped to the ground and a volley of boots and fists rained down on his head and body. During the beating itself he felt immune to the pain, and at first none of the blows seemed to have any physical impact, but as the shock of being assaulted subsided in the hours and days afterwards, his ribs ached, his jaw throbbed and whenever he went for a shower he noticed the cuts and bruises marking his body. The mental wounds were more severe, however. For a year, Malcolm was unable to attend a game of football without experiencing a minor breakdown. (It probably didn't help that he was a Luton Town fan.) He felt unsettled in large groups of people. Whenever there was a loud noise, he was nervous and fearful – even if the sound carried a positive association. Malcolm told me that whenever Luton Town scored and the people around him celebrated loudly, his anxiety skyrocketed.

Malcolm's mind was in a phase of intense self-protection because his brain had stored a recording of what the attack had felt like. Whenever he was at a football game, he became hyper-vigilant, overly aware that a physical assault was possible. Psychologically, Malcolm was now conditioned to experience fear, and his new emotional injury was acting as a warning sign: *Mate, you could get badly hurt here – you might even die if things get really out of hand.* If I were to simplify his experience, I'd say Malcolm's brain was acting like a crashing comparison website search engine; it had taken an unpleasant past experience and it was drawing parallels to the now, and every football match he attended recalled the memory of bruising pain.

Luckily, Malcolm was in a position to seek help. As a younger man he'd experienced several tricky personal issues until a period of professional emotional counselling turned his life around. He was no stranger to the type of therapy required for healing in the aftermath of his assault and he happily went into a period of recovery. Eventually, Malcolm was able to heal to the point where he could watch a football match again without stress or any fear of attack. The broken comparison website search engine had been fixed; Malcolm had unlearned his fears. Once sorted, Malcolm became interested in learning more about therapy's emotional benefits. This eventually led him to become a therapist himself and he often helps others to work through anxieties and traumas of their own.

#2 Anger

This is one of the most distressing and dangerous symptoms of an emotionally frazzled person – both for the individual involved and the people around them. Sufferers become unpredictable and volatile. At the low end of the problem, they might develop unusual shifts in body language – for example, a psychoactivity that manifests as a nervous tic, or twitch. At the high end, they become violent and incredibly short-tempered, emotionally racing from zero to a hundred miles per hour at the first sign of a flashpoint. These people are sometimes dangerous to be around. I know, because once or twice I veered towards the high end at the peak of my own emotional distress. I didn't become actively violent, but I had a short fuse and at times I fantasized about doing some damage to one or two annoying colleagues in a civilian job I'd taken. Luckily, I was able to keep control of this.

So, where does the anger come from? Well, rage is the obvious 'fight' in a fight-or-flight response, a surge of adrenaline that primes the body for action. Even the digestive system is temporarily switched off in order to give the person all the power they'll require to survive in a conflict or retreat. Problems arise when there's no real danger to rail against and the anger is used as a disproportionate response to an everyday situation, such as a minor dispute over a restaurant meal or a domestic tiff. In those situations, the person suffering from mental distress will flare up to a point where they become incredibly aggressive, or worse. As with hyper-vigilance, the mind reacts to a normal event in an extreme way because it hasn't rationalized the initial source of trauma.

This response is particularly common in people unlucky enough to encounter hardcore violence, as many people do when working in the military or emergency services, where all sorts of grim situations unfold. Although people functioning in these roles are highly trained to deal with outbreaks of extreme behaviour, the consequences of social disorder or the sort of injuries that can occur in high-impact accidents or fires, they're still human. They have tolerance limits like everybody else. And if an individual's tolerance limit is broken, the person breaks, too. When life has been rendered almost insignificant, in a war zone or crime scene, it becomes a challenge to return to a normal, family environment.

In the emotionally injured, anger also arises out of habit. While elite operators are expected to control their emotions, the brain still responds in ways that nudge us towards extreme behaviour (though we understand the importance of keeping a lid on this). For everyone else, however, anger can become a reflex response to certain situations, like the anxiety experienced by Malcolm at football matches; it's habitual because it's set off by fear. That habit has been borne in understandable circumstances, such as within military conflict, but when the individual affected is then placed in a safer environment, they're unable to differentiate between risk and routine. The slightest challenge becomes a call to extreme action. Think of it in terms of someone who has been bitten by a pit bull terrier. If they tend to go into a panic every time they see a dog in the street, it's because they've developed a fearful sensitivity to a type of animal that's previously caused them serious harm. Similarly, a person that once associated shouting and loud noises with military combat – or, in Malcolm's case, football-related violence – might struggle to shrug off those emotions when any shouting or loud noises happen at home or in the street.

When we're born, our emotional system works perfectly. In fact, we arrive with only two fears: of loud noises and falling. In

1960, 'The Visual Cliff' – a study of babies aged six to fourteen months old – determined that the fear of falling was a survival mechanism instilled in us all at birth. (Though the report doesn't claim to prove the fear is innate, the author's tests on animals suggested that it is. This study might also explain why I first developed my fear of heights, but it doesn't give a reason for why I wasn't able to overcome that fear as a kid while my mates could.) Meanwhile, loud noises trigger our fight-or-flight response from day one, thanks to our 'acoustic startle reflex', and it's the reason we jump during films or when a plate crashes to the floor. According to Seth Norrholm, a translational neuroscientist from Emory University, Georgia, this circuitry is 'innate'. Other than that, we're like a new smartphone, psychologically at least – box fresh, with unaltered factory settings. Over time, life experiences change those settings in different ways, and at their most extreme, certain events can cause neurological damage. Our systems crash.

Trauma of shocking proportions, such as losing a mate in horrible circumstances, has the potential to cause so much damage that the emotional wounds might take a long time to heal, if at all. Unless help is called in, these wounds can leave permanent scars, eventually causing the victim's hard drive to freeze. When people have flashbacks to shocking life-incidents, it's because their system has crashed and they're unable to process the incident. The lessons they needed to draw from the moment go unlearned and can't be stored as intel for future decision-making responses. Worse, whatever's taken place seems to float in their immediate consciousness, constantly gnawing at the edges of their thinking.

Calling for emotional reinforcements is the only way forward.

#3 Numbness (and the Inability to Ask for Help)

It's common for the partner of an emotionally wounded individual to be the first to approach us at Rock2Recovery, and often this can be a heart-breaking introduction.

'He's emotionally numb,' they'll say. 'He can't even deal with the kids laughing. I don't know what to do about it.'

Or, 'She's not the same person that went away. She won't even communicate with me. It's like she's a ghost.'

Psychological numbness is an extreme reaction to a highly emotional event. In times of heavy distress, the brain loads up on what could be described as emotional anaesthesia. It administers doses of mental painkillers in order to silence the anguish that's taken place. This is an act of self-protection: if the person can't *feel*, they won't *hurt* any more. But without feeling, people become oblivious to their predicament. They know something's not right emotionally, but they're unable to comprehend or express exactly what's wrong. Numbness then crushes them and everyone moving within their orbit.

One step towards recovery is for a therapist to detach an individual from their initial trauma through a series of disassociation techniques. This process allows the client to fully understand their experience without the usual negative emotional response. Eventually it's an incident that can be recalled without pain, panic or grief; with work, they'll 'watch' rather than 'live' the moment, like a film or TV show, until it's ultimately reduced to basic information. To illustrate the process, here's an extract from a transcript of a session with a Rock2Recovery therapist and an individual who had experienced a violent, potentially life-threatening assault thirty years previously. We'll call the person involved Client X. (The assault wasn't the cause of their trauma and Client X happily agreed to their transcript being used for the purpose of this book.)

Client X was beaten up in a violent mugging on a packed bus. Knives were put to his throat; another knifepoint was stuck at his back. The assailants stole his money, trainers, belt and jumper. At the time, he was fourteen years old and he recalls feeling 'angry' that no one stepped in to help him. For a while, the incident affected him greatly. His schoolwork suffered and he felt vulnerable. He says the upside, however, was that the attack gave him a sixth sense. 'Where previously I would have been naive about certain situations, it taught me when to be on my guard,' he said.

During their meeting, the therapist employed what he and Malcolm Williams have described as the 'Doctor Who' technique. Having listened to Client X's description of the event, the therapist asked him to mentally revisit the experience as he was then, a naive fourteen-year-old kid on a night out with mates. He then asked Client X to reframe the incident, returning to it not as a teenager but as a forty-something bloke, picturing the scene in the clothes he was wearing that day for his counselling session. In effect, he was asking Client X to project his current self on to a past experience to see what emotional differences he might notice.

'I use the TV character Doctor Who as a metaphor,' explained the counsellor. 'So Doctor Who gets in the Tardis with his assistant. They set the controls of the Tardis and they time-travel. And let's say it's 2025 and they time-travel back to 1990, so they go back in time thirty-five years. When they step out of the

Tardis they're exactly the same people, in the same clothes that they were wearing in 2025. They don't regress. If Doctor Who is fifty years old when he steps into the Tardis, he doesn't become fifteen by travelling back thirty-five years. But metaphorically, that's what happens when we go back to an unhealed memory: we go back to the time that it happened as the person we were then. Someone who was a child-abuse victim might be forty now but neurologically, whenever they think about it, they suffer the experience as a six-year-old.'

When asked to describe the differences he was noticing, Client X claimed he would have acted more rationally during the heat of the moment. Rather than putting up a fight – an action that led to him being beaten up – he would have worked harder to maintain his composure. 'I'd say, "Right, what is it you want? The money? Have it . . ."' said Client X. 'They had knives! Instead, I put up a struggle, which is what got me the beating. With hindsight, I could have been a bit more pragmatic because there were moments where I thought, *I'm going to get my face carved open here.*

'With hindsight it's much easier to rationalize the situation and think, *Well, in terms of value, what's been taken? A hundred and fifty pounds' – worth of clothes and money? In the grand scheme of things, who cares?* I wouldn't have wanted any of my mates, or someone stepping in, to have got stabbed or seriously hurt for a hundred and fifty pounds.'

'So look at the difference,' said the therapist. 'You go back in your white shoes, your black jeans and your grey top of today, rather than what you were wearing back then. You're Client X in the here and now, and you have a new perspective: you're seeing it using all the wisdom you've accrued since then to view the situation differently. The narrow focus you were using for the trauma has opened out into a wide focus. You can see the difference in the way you're thinking about it when you go back wearing today's clothes as the older, more experienced you . . .'

Techniques of this kind might sound unorthodox to people who haven't experienced therapy before, but they act as an effective desensitizing exercise for tackling a traumatic incident, such as the mugging described by Client X. This is only a snapshot of a wider counselling programme, though; one step in a series of efforts to help a person tackle their emotional problems head-on. And don't be fooled by the easiness of the conversation detailed here: going into a period of recovery of this kind takes guts and resilience. It's a hard challenge, in pretty much the same way that rehabilitating from a serious injury takes courage, time and effort, too. People going into this process should be respected for their bravery.

It's worth noting that techniques of this kind can help us to understand less traumatic events in our lives as well. Perhaps we're still scarred by an argument that led to a major falling-out with a close friend or a loved one. Maybe we've suffered as a result of a financial decision that was made in the past and we're unable to emotionally reconcile with our mistakes. Or it could be that we're still angry about a decision that impacted on our lives in an unpleasant way. Projecting our current self – with all the knowledge, wisdom and resilience accrued in the meantime – is a good way to shake off some emotional baggage. It also helps us to psychologically prepare for our reactions should a similar event take place in the future.

*

At this point in the book you might be thinking, *I've just read a chapter on emotional breakdown and failure. That hardly suggests the author has a resilient mindset.* Or, *This bloke nearly killed himself through PTSD. Is he really the best person to talk to me about emotional fortitude?* Fair points. Except, my experience makes me *exactly* the kind of person you should be listening to. I've witnessed the horrors of hardcore military service, crash-landed at a mental low and doubted the value of my life – yet still, somehow, I've been able to turn myself around. If the very definition of resilience is the 'ability to return quickly from illness, change, or misfortune', then I have an intense understanding of that experience.

The bottom line is this: we all have the potential to rebound from failure as a better, stronger, more resilient individual but a system reset takes time, care and bravery, as I've discovered. Handily, recovering from an emotional wound can be approached in the same way that we've treated every other challenge within *Life Under Fire*. Use the Commando Spirit. Recall your purpose. Push through the Fear Zone and into periods of learning and growth. Bring your brotherhood around you. Be brutally honest with yourself and become increasingly self-aware.

Most of all though, it's important to remember that even the best operators get wounded in gunfights. If you're badly injured, the smartest move is to call in a CASEVAC for medical treatment because the fight isn't over yet. And once repaired and ready to return, an elite soldier can expect to jump back into battle, to serve as a viable asset once more. The same applies to you: regardless of the conflict or challenge, when bleeding out, ask for help. With this assistance, you can live to fight another day.

OPERATIONAL DEBRIEF

» We all break at one point or another – it's part of being human. By asking for help or calling in reinforcements, you'll live to fight another day.

» Learn your emotional combat indicators. How do you behave when life is spiralling out of control? Make a note of any behavioural responses to alert yourself to an approaching break point.

» Recognize the symptoms of rock bottom: hyper-vigilance, disproportionate anger and a numb, detached attitude. Know these signs not only in yourself but in the people around you.

» No matter your problem or psychological injury, there is someone who can – and will – help. However, therapists are like accountants and dentists – there are thousands and thousands of them and each one is individual. Having summoned up the courage to seek help, don't be afraid to shop around. Counselling is an incredibly personal experience and you should look for someone you feel comfortable with.

SITUATIONAL AWARENESS

SHELVE YOUR EGO
FOR THE GREATER GOOD

Asking for help might require you to lose face, but go ahead and do it anyway. Remember that each of us takes a fall from time to time and it's part of the human experience. Functioning with a stiff upper lip while keeping calm and carrying on might work in some circumstances, but when it comes to matters of mental health, raising a hand for help is the best way forward. *But it's hard.*

One method for leaping over that psychological hurdle is to shelve your ego. For too long I placed myself and my self-image on a pedestal. *I'm Jason Fox, former elite operator; I captured some seriously dangerous people in scary places. I survived war zones and I came through Selection. I can't be broken.* This attitude is transferable to other occupations, such as business. *I'm a company director. I set this firm up from nothing and turned it into a multimillion-pound company. For years I worked sixteen-hour days, seven days a week, without holidays. I can't be broken.* With inflexible attitudes like these, the crashes are bloody painful when they happen.

One way of resolving this problem is for an individual to separate their reputation, career achievements and abilities from their actual person – the Real Them. For example, when the successful businesswoman arrives home after a day in charge, where everyone works to her demands, she might get a shock: the kids won't behave, her partner needs to talk through a personal disagreement and the bills have all arrived at once. Suddenly she's not the boss of the boardroom any more.

If she allows her ego to get in the way, it might be difficult for her to behave in an appropriate and effective manner. Talking to her kids like a disruptive colleague won't give them the love and education they need. Shouting at her partner as if they're another frustrating supplier will only cause a terrible rift. Expecting family life to move to the same rhythm as her successful career is unrealistic and a fast route to conflict. Instead, she needs to remember the Real Her, because her achievements and career goals won't help her to maintain emotional stability, no matter what the ego says.

This technique was vital to me when asking for help after hitting rock bottom. I had to separate my achievements, reputation and abilities in the military from Jason Fox, son, brother, father – the Real Me – before I could summon the courage to get help. The healing started once I'd stopped telling myself, *I'm Jason Fox, former elite operator . . . I can't be broken.* That's not to say I forgot those achievements. I didn't; they're still very important to me and I'm proud of them. Rather, I shelved my ego when I needed to do something for my greater good, like asking for help in a time of emotional trauma.

There isn't a single human being on the planet that doesn't break down. *Not one.* But how we respond to our personal conflicts is what defines us. Remembering that there's a difference between our real selves and how our ego needs us to be seen is a very effective way of overcoming any emotional resistance when calling in reinforcements.

PHASE TWELVE

THE RELOAD: FINDING
YOUR YUKON

So how do we regroup after an emotional blowout?

Following my medical discharge from the military, I'd under-standably lost my edge, but finding that strength and sharpness again was a process I eventually became excited by.

My healing process began with therapy, which took place during a series of walks through the woods near my counsellor's office, because she'd recognized the calming effect the outdoors had on me. I later took that idea of working in nature to extremes as I rebuilt my life. Row-ing across the Atlantic with Team Essence was the first step. I then embraced more and more challenges, continually stepping out of my comfort zone with each one, and embarking on missions that truly drew together the five building blocks of resilience.

A recent example of this was my 2019 kayak expedition along the Yukon River in a two-man, unsupported mission with Sean John-son, an experienced adventurer who had previously travelled down the Mississippi, Missouri and Rhine Rivers. Sean had also taken a winter hike along the entire length of the Appalachian Trail and cycled across Canada from east to west. In expedition terms, he was a serious player. But by leaning in to purpose, experience, brotherhood, self-awareness and honesty, we were able to overcome the hurdles placed in our path, as I'll explain over the following pages.

Everybody has an adventure to execute. Start with courage and commitment, and the rest will follow.

For the remainder of Phase Twelve, the five building blocks of resilience are detailed in the order in which they were implemented during the expedition. As I've mentioned previously, purpose, experience, brotherhood, self-awareness and honesty are equally important and work concurrently. It's not necessary to apply them in a particular order.

STEP #1
PURPOSE AND THE NEXT ADVENTURE

Am I still suffering from PTSD?

It's a question a lot of people have asked me since I pieced my life back together, especially after my admission on *SAS: Who Dares Wins* and in response to *Battle Scars*. The honest answer is that I'm doing great and those emotional stresses don't weigh me down any more. I'm not saying I won't suffer from those symptoms again because an unexpected life-event might shove me back into that hole, but these days I'm much more resistant to emotional turbulence. I have the tools to overcome whatever shit life chucks at me, and if ever I do find myself feeling down, I make sure to give that moment, *that emotion*, the respect it deserves.

I'll ask myself, *Why do I feel like this?* Then, having acknowledged the feelings that have put me in a bit of a dip, I'll do whatever I can to mentally course-correct. I work out, or check in with mates. Maybe I'll plan another expedition or project. These are the processes that help to maintain my emotional even-keel. Their impacts can be either immediate or slow-moving, but they're always positive.

Over a few years, it eventually became apparent that my purpose had changed. My new focus was self-improvement – both for myself and others. We're all different, though. It's important that, through the phases we've discussed in the book so far, you identify your own positive physical and emotional responses to setbacks and problems. *Your own 'why'*. Mine was to throw myself into a gritty challenge set against the backdrop of a testing environment.

Kayaking down the Yukon River in Canada and America, from source to sea, had long been an ambition of mine, as it had for Sean. There was adventure – *purpose*. As an extra incentive, I used the expedition as a fundraising event for Rock2Recovery, the Special Boat Service Association and the Royal Marines Charity. I was also looking forward to reconnecting with nature. A lot of the work I'd loved the most had involved being out in the wild, whether that was while operating with the British military or when thrashing recruits in the jungle during *SAS: Who Dares Wins*. I felt switched on in the great outdoors. The challenge was set to be exhilarating. *There was purpose in adventure. There was purpose in charity. There was purpose in working with Sean.* With such a powerful set of motives, every pull of the paddle came loaded with incentive.

STEP #2
EXPERIENCE AND THE BIG WIDE OPEN

The work was mega-honking from the off. To prepare for the trip, we'd readied our kit in the UK and tested the kayaks on local rivers and in the sea; it was important to become familiar with the rhythms of the water and how the boat might sit within it. But before we were even able to get in the kayaks, we had to walk forty-nine miles from our starting point at Skagway to Bennett – one of the Yukon's suspected sources, where the river was nothing more than a trickle. (The widely accepted source of the Yukon is the Llewellyn Glacier, though some people claim it might be Lake Lindeman too.) But this was only the warm-up phase. A train was due to meet us with our kayaks before we paddled along the Yukon's entire length, all 1,980 miles of it, until we reached the Bering Sea.

The trekking route was intense; the terrain was uncomfortable and we covered at least ten miles per day while carrying around 100lb of kit in our rucksacks, which included our comms kit and all the basics we needed for the trip, such as a tent, sleeping bags and cooking equipment.

My feet were in agony every night, but I leaned into the experience I'd gathered during past expeditions. When I'd rowed the Atlantic, I found it quite daunting to imagine the trip as a whole, especially when I was in physical pain. Rowing from Portugal to Venezuela on a route comprising 3,308 nautical miles and seven weeks at sea was an intimidating prospect, so I decided to mentally break it down into smaller stages, such as the legs between the Canary Islands and Africa, or Africa to the Azores. Once we'd completed each phase I ticked it off in my head and marked it as an achievement, all the while visualizing the success of completing the trip in world-record-setting time. I pictured the crew – Aldo Kane, Ross Johnson, Oliver Bailey, Mathew Bennett and I – celebrating with beers in our boat, the *Elida*, as we docked at Macuro. The image kept me going whenever the vessel was capsizing or as I huddled alongside Aldo for warmth, the elements having battered the boat and flooded the sleeping cabin. This was a vital learning moment that I later shared during a number of talks and podcasts. I even returned to Lympstone to chat with Commando wannabes as they worked through the Potential Royal Marines Course, and explained how the visualization processes I'd used during the Atlantic row could be applied to the experience of becoming a Royal Marine.

'Picture yourself wearing that beret at the end,' I said. 'Think about it, *visualize it*. You can see yourself getting it, can't you? Right, push that to the back of your head – don't forget it, just keep it there. Now, break the course into small pieces, deal with every day as it presents itself . . .'

It helped to put my own ideas into practice every now and then. As we walked, I imagined Sean and myself pushing away from land for the first time in our kayaks. Visualizing the gentle swell of water around me as we paddled into the unknown also helped. I even fantasized about the cigar and the whiskies I was going to enjoy at the end of our trip. This mental process motivated me as we trekked along what is known as the Chilkoot Trail, and after four days of walking – with the last stretch a hellish few miles of sand dunes – the town of Bennett came into view. Both of us had been thrashed. Most people took over a week to complete that same trail, hiking at a leisurely pace.

'That was the hardest thing I've done for a long time,' said Sean later.

Shortly afterwards we were in our kayaks, the three lakes of Bennett, Tagish and Marsh ahead of us, the heavy currents of the Yukon beyond. The clouds were sweeping in overhead. The waves around us were building. I looked around and smiled.

Bloody hell, this is all right, I thought.

The good vibes wouldn't last for long.

STEP #3
HONESTY AND NEAR-DEATH

We pushed through shitshow after shitshow on the water, each time acknowledging we were in trouble while working hard to un-fuck our situation with positive action. The hiccups were never-ending. By the second day, Sean's rudder had snapped away and water was leaking into his kayak. We tried to block the hole ourselves but with very little luck, and Sean was soon wasting vital energy pulling over to the bank so he could empty the boat. The water was bloody freezing.

We limped our way to a small town called Carcross at the end of Lake Bennett, where we patched up the damage with some superglue and a few rolls of duct tape before pushing through our first storm. By nightfall we were piss-wet through and exhausted. We'd been on the water for sixteen hours.

For the first week or so of paddling, we were strong enough to put away a hundred kilometres per day, but the work was physically bruising, and as time went on we became increasingly fatigued and our progress was much slower. Having finally closed in on Emmonak, the last town on our route before reaching the Bering Sea, we were then scuppered by an incoming storm. I'd felt it building behind us and the waves were growing; whitecaps churned in the distance and there was no way we'd outrun the heavy rain. The light was fading, too. *It was time to make a brutally honest assessment.* We accepted this minor defeat and recognized its value as an opportunity to rest.

'We're not going to make it to Emmonak tonight,' said Sean. 'We'll do it tomorrow. We need to get off the water.'

It was annoying, but at least we weren't going to get sucked into the Yukon as a result of our exhaustion.

Sean and I had long decided to camp on islands or sandbars because the chances of stumbling into the local grizzly bears were much slimmer away from the mainland. The only suitable spot in sight was a small bank of land in the middle of the river. After a brief discussion, we pressed towards it; once we'd made it, we waited until the rain and winds subsided.

Not that our troubles ended on terra firma. There were no trees on the island; everything was exposed to the elements and the wind howled around us. Putting up the tent was almost impossible, and once we'd crawled inside everything was soaked through, even the sleeping bags. We rustled up a quick hot drink, chowed down on some beef jerky and tried to sleep as the storm battered the sodden frame of our shelter. Every half an hour, one of us unzipped the tent door to check on the water levels and the whereabouts of the kayaks, which we'd positioned in a V-shape in front of the tent to form a makeshift windbreak. At 5.30 a.m., with the sun yet to come up, Sean took his turn as lookout.

He nudged me awake. 'Mate, we're leaving – *now*.'

What the fuck?

'There's a surge coming in – the island's flooding. If we don't get a move on, we're going to get swept away.'

I looked outside. Sean was right; the scene was pretty ugly. The water had crept closer and closer towards us, like a fast-moving tide on a beach. Moving frantically, we collapsed the camp, and as we sat in our boats, shivering, waiting for the swell to draw us back into the chaos, it was hard not to feel despondent. I was freezing and my kit was soaked through; the tent was in ribbons and our plans had been torn to shreds. But there was no point wallowing in what might have been or how bad our predicament had become. Positive action was the only way to stay alive.

STEP #4
SELF-AWARENESS IN A FLOOD

Special Forces training had taught me that in situations of this kind, my survival hinged on flexibility. Sean and I were paddling back into the conditions we'd been trying so desperately to avoid a few hours earlier, but the chances of escape now seemed even slimmer. We were still being battered by high winds; choppy swells smashed into the boats, over and over again. Our position was a small dot in a very big expanse of water, and the Yukon was around four miles wide at that point. I looked down at our digital map.

'Mate, the river eventually narrows to about a kilometre in width, but it's about two kilometres' worth of paddling to get there.'

Sean nodded. 'Let's fucking go for it. We've got to do something. We can't hang here – we'll die.'

I looked out at the water. Huge waves loomed ahead. The wind whipped across the water. I was scared.

'Right, are we doing this?' said Sean.

I nodded. *Yeah.*

'OK. It's going to be twenty minutes of hard graft,' he said. 'But we've got to go for it.'

Thanks to self-awareness, I knew there would be fear; the situation demanded it, really, but I was at least ready for any moments where my emotions might overwhelm me. Controlling any anxieties at that stage was vital. If I became emotionally spun out at any point, it might prevent me from functioning effectively, and if that was for only a split second it could have been the difference between making it to Emmonak for an elk burger and a bottle of whisky or a grim death at the bottom of the Yukon.

As we moved on, each wave threatened to flip us over. Being positioned only a few inches off the water in a kayak made the experience incredibly intimidating; there were times when I was absolutely petrified. Every rise and fall of the tide forced me to steady my craft, and there was also the reality of the water I was working in. It was heavy with silt. I'd heard rumours of people going into the Yukon and, because their clothing quickly filled with sediment, they were unable to break above the water's surface. When I looked up at Sean again, he, too, was operating in his own little world, scrapping to stay alive.

'This is serious,' he shouted. 'If one of us goes in, how's the other one going to help? We're each in a fucking kayak!'

I tried to stay calm. *Concentrate on what you need to do*, I thought, recalling the One Metre Square theory. *Don't go over. Do not fucking capsize. Remember everything you've learned over the last 1,500 miles . . .*

I hadn't been that close to death for quite some time. I was being flipped around in an emotional roller coaster, and a split second of doubt inevitably flickered across my mind. *This is fucking horrendous. We could die here.* Then I settled myself again, pulling my stresses into the One Metre Square around me. I focused only on the immediate seconds ahead. *You won't capsize. And if you don't capsize, you won't die. Concentrate on what needs to be done. Concentrate on not giving up.* In other situations, I'd used that resilient mindset to push myself on, such as in the mix of a terrifying gun battle. Back then I'd thought, *I need to switch on a little bit. The way I'm going to get out of here is to start shooting, do whatever I need to do . . .* It had kept me alive in the past; it would keep me alive now.

'Mate!' I heard Sean shouting at me from across the water. He was gesticulating to a small inlet in the shoreline. It looked like a lagoon area where a group of fallen trees had been deposited by the fast-moving Yukon. On one side, violent waves slapped into the log pile, but a pond of still water had formed behind them.

'We need to get into that,' he yelled, changing course and charging for the riverbank.

I followed his tail until we'd reached what looked like a small, natural dam. We pulled our kayaks inside. It wasn't an ideal situation. The area was surrounded by head-high vegetation and a pathway had been flattened down at the back, probably by animals using the space as a watering hole.

Bears.

STEP #5
BROTHERHOOD AT THE LOWEST EBB

We'd already been bumped once by a grizzly bear on the trip and it hadn't been pleasant. While resting on a sandbank one day, drying our kit and eating some lunch, Sean had suddenly looked up.

'I can see something moving over there,' he said, pointing. 'It's either a moose or a bear. I'm not sure which.'

Sean moved closer to get eyes on the target. Seconds later he was running towards the boats, waving at me to do the same.

'It's a bloody grizzly! Get into the kayak!'

I sprinted to the shoreline, grabbing my sleeping bag and as much of our equipment as I could carry, while 800lb of fur, teeth and claws advanced on our position. The bear had sniffed our food and was now approaching at speed; Sean and I headed out into the middle of the Yukon, watching as the beast rummaged through what was left of our camp. Once we were certain it was done, we made a quick return, grabbing the last pieces of kit and paddling away.

I didn't fancy a repeat experience at our new temporary base, but there was nowhere else to go. Wading into the waist-high water, we wedged our boats into the watering hole access point and set up camp on the bank. The tent was battered after several weeks in the wild. Meanwhile, the Yukon had soaked everything during the storm – our clothes, our sleeping bags, even our food. The inflatable mats we'd been sleeping on were fucked too. Our moment of weakness had arrived and we were both emotionally vulnerable, but our military training had readied us for events such as this one. The important thing was to acknowledge the reality of our situation. *What the fuck have we got ourselves into?* Then take stock of where we were and accept our very human response. *This is fucking scary and not nice.* To ignore those feelings, or to pretend that everything was OK, might have led to denial and then failure. Once we'd gathered our thoughts, it was time to push away any negative emotion.

I respected Sean. He'd been through plenty of grim situations in a kayak on all sorts of expeditions and was regarded as being highly experienced within the Royal Marines, where he'd learned the importance of resilience and the Commando Spirit. When life became sketchy, he understood how to stop himself from caving in. Meanwhile, both of us knew we could trust one another; just as I'd experienced in the military elite, there was an unwritten agreement that we were in this as a team, no matter how desperate our situation became. I could lean on Sean; Sean could lean on me. Despite the cold and the wet, not to mention the stress of having to make it to Emmonak before our flight home departed, I understood I was exactly where I'd wanted to be: operating outside of my comfort zone and working within a brotherhood.

I grabbed some peanut butter and bread and loaded up a couple of sandwiches, before figuring out the next move.

OK, what's going on?

'We're good for time,' said Sean. 'It's a squeeze, but we'll be OK. The issue is this fucking storm raging around us . . .'

We decided to wait for a bit, eventually crawling into our sodden sleeping bags. Hoping the storm might die off overnight, we made plans to move quickly to Emmonak as soon as we could. As for our survival? Well, paddling in the dark wasn't ideal, but at least it was something. *And then I remembered.*

'Mate, wait there!' I said, wading back out to my kayak in the icy-cold water. I searched through the back of the boat until I'd laid hands on a tube of Pringles – my break-in-case-of-emergency rations. The packaging was banged up a bit and the cardboard was soggy, but the crisps inside were fairly dry thanks to the lining. Sean's eyes lit up as I flipped the top open and offered him a stack of salty treats.

'Once you pop, mate . . .'

'You can't stop,' laughed Sean.

Emotionally, we had turned the corner by acknowledging our feelings and finding humour in adversity. The response was like one of those power surges from a shoot-'em-up video game. Resting for the night in our sodden sleeping bags, the winds buffeting the tent, we drifted off to sleep to the music from one of our mobile phones. Every now and then I'd check on the weather, hoping for some small improvement, but the conditions were unrelenting.

Having dozed off again, I was woken by Sean. It was morning. He was shaking me.

'Mate, we're getting up.'

What? Why?

I propped myself up on an elbow and felt it: beneath me, the ground was moving, as if we were sleeping on a waterbed. The river had swept in around us. We were floating.

'The bank's flooded,' said Sean. 'We've got to pack up and get into the boats.'

Moments later, the pair of us were back in the water again, paddling away from our camp into the choppy currents of the Yukon. *What a drama.* The winds were still high and, even though it was fairly calm in our secluded lagoon, I could see the river was nightmarishly rough as I led us away.

'How does it look out there?' asked Sean as I turned the corner.

It was bad. I really didn't want to move out, but our options were limited. Sean shook his head.

'In my experience, those waves are still too big,' he said. 'I'm not happy at all.'

For a brief moment, I wondered whether we were all out of options. We were pretty helpless, and unsure of how long the storm was going to last. But there was one person I knew who might have a handle on what to do next. *Dad.* He lived on a boat in the Mediterranean, and had a pretty good understanding of storm tracking and global weather systems. I punched his number into my satellite phone and hoped for the best. Eventually, after one or two attempts, we were connected.

'Dad, there's a storm in the Emmonak area and we're trapped,' I said. 'I need to know what's going on.'

There was a pause. 'Give me fifteen minutes to check,' he said. 'Call me back then.'

A quarter of an hour later we had a fuller picture of the situation we were facing. The storm was big – really big. But the good news was that we'd already seen out most of it.

'The winds are going to die down a bit between two and three o'clock in the afternoon,' said Dad. 'They'll still be strong, but by seven tonight you'll be fine.'

Even though we were around half a day away from the finishing line, a little light had appeared at the end of the tunnel. And it turned out that we didn't have to wait that long: having got through the morning, by one in the afternoon the storm was settling down enough for us to consider pushing off again. Sean and I perched on the edge of the river in our kayaks, staring at the churning water ahead. He wanted to know if I was ready for the upcoming test.

'Fuck it,' I said. 'Let's go for it. We're only twelve kilometres from the finish.'

Sean nodded. The journey was set to be grim work, but both of us were ready. I was in charge of our GPS, and Sean had an idea to help us through the final stage.

'Every time we clock off a kilometre, I want you to shout it out,' he said.

Yeah! One hundred per cent.

We paddled out and powered into the storm. As every kilometre passed, I shouted out to Sean over the gale.

One kilometre!

Two kilometres!

I must have sounded like the Count from *Sesame Street* until, eventually, the fishing village of Emmonak came into sight. We were safe.

According to the Fun Scale – a quantifiable measurement of

exciting activities – there are three types of 'enjoyable' events in life. Type One is the quick buzz: a piss-up with friends, a cracking night out, or the winning goal in an important football match. It tends to be a brief surge of dopamine that doesn't really last that long and usually leaves a person wanting more of the same. Type Two is very different. It is an experience or challenge that feels utterly miserable, or disorientating in the moment – such as an ultramarathon or a long-distance rowing race – but once completed, the pain is slowly forgotten and a glow of achievement takes over. It often feels as though life has changed for the better as a result and before long, a desire to repeat the experience, or to go one further, kicks in. Type Three is the worst of the lot: a painful experience that is a constant threat to life and requires a rescue attempt at the end.

Travelling the Yukon River fell into the Type Two category.

As we finally dragged ourselves from the water, two local blokes approached us. They were sizing up our battered kayaks.

'Are you selling those?' asked one.

Too fucking right I am. I'm not taking this thing home.

I took the cash, but my sour mood didn't last for long. Thanks to the unusual nature of Type-Two fun, I was soon revelling in every near-death moment on the Yukon, even before I'd made the long flight home. There were times when one of us could have died, but I'd been able to manage my emotions, maintaining a resilient spirit until the end. I had fulfilled my purpose and thrived in a newfound sense of brotherhood with Sean. I had felt fear, but I'd survived, learned, and then grown. The experience had made me more resilient than ever before.

The demons had been silenced yet again.

OPERATIONAL DEBRIEF

» To remain emotionally strong, engage with projects that are mentally and physically challenging. The Yukon expedition gave me purpose: there was the opportunity to raise money for charity while working in an intimidating environment alongside a good mate.

» Break down intimidating events into manageable targets rather than imagining the whole thing. During the gruelling trek to the water, I visualized the endgame: a scene of Sean and me sitting in our kayaks on Lake Bennett, the still water gently swelling around us. In the closing stage of the river journey, we mentally checked off every kilometre as an accomplishment.

» Use self-awareness to ready yourself for fear. I was in a situation where unease was understandable – there was no point denying it. Rather than crumbling, I used the fear to concentrate, negotiating the incoming waves one by one.

» Sometimes the only way to survive is to acknowledge the severity of the situation and work towards finding a solution through positive action. At no point did Sean or I grumble about the shit we were stuck in – not for too long, anyway. We tried to make jokes while remaining proactive.

» Prepare for any emotional lows with a break-in-case-of-emergency reward. If we're working abroad for a long time, we should pack some home comforts for any heavy moments. In the middle of a gruelling project, factor in a night off for relaxing. In the midst of an emotional life-event, take an hour or so to walk outside listening to music or a podcast.

SITUATIONAL AWARENESS

BEWARE THE FALSE ENDING

In war, missions and gunfights rarely run on the clock. Battles don't end at sundown only to start up again once it gets light; people don't check out of contact situations for a rest. I've been in scraps that have lasted for over thirty-six hours, and I was physically and emotionally rinsed by the end of each one. Every battle has its own rhythm and tempo, too. Sometimes the shooting can be relentless, the bullets landing from all angles in a seemingly never-ending barrage. At other times, the contact becomes sporadic – an enemy target might fire off a few bursts, only to move positions and then start up again when it's least expected. The trick was to stay on high-alert at all times.

During the Yukon expedition, there were moments when I'd believed a storm was blowing itself out, only for the winds to flare up again minutes later. Or it might have felt as though our final destination for the day was in sight, when it was actually around another large bend in the river. Without mental strength, those disappointments can feel demoralizing.

Luckily, experience of these situations was instilled in me during my military service. During courses, instructors would run drills for hours on end and then create a situation where it seemed as if our work was winding down for the day – but this turned out to be a trick. As the lads settled down and mentally prepared for a rest and a wet, the action suddenly started up again, out of nowhere. The effect was unsettling, but also informative. It taught me that when the mind switched off, the body was at its most vulnerable. I had to be constantly alert and ready for anything.

False endings appear in life all the time. We think our workload on a project has come to an end, only for an issue or glitch to arise unexpectedly, putting us back a few days, or even weeks. An illness or injury might take longer to recover from than the original diagnosis had suggested. Having become emotionally blown off-course by a life-event, we might need more time than usual to power up to full strength, or motivate ourselves. The only way to handle these false endings is to ready ourselves for them even when it might seem unnecessary. When assessing the finishing line, we should adjust our resources for a worst-case scenario or, at the very least, a slight problem at the end. For example:

- Plan your end-of-deadline celebration a couple of days after the closing date, just in case.
- Regularly run, swim, climb or cycle a distance longer than the race you'll be competing in. As a result, you'll

have much more left in the emotional tank in the closing stages.

- Shock the body by getting your training mate to randomly throw in another set of exercises at the end of a gym session, especially when you're already feeling knackered.

Because the battle is never truly over until you're home, safe, and ready to go again.

ENDGAME

Resilience is a skill. And like any skill, it takes time and effort to maintain. Repetition and practice are important. If we don't regularly challenge ourselves, our resistance to adversity can wane and our skills fade. One early example of this struck me during my thirties. As a kid, I'd been a pretty good hockey player and, having made it into the Royal Marines, I represented the regiment in a number of inter-services tournaments, both at home and abroad. Once I'd passed Selection and started operating in the Special Forces, however, showing up for competitions was off the table so hockey fell by the wayside. That was until 2010, when a mate asked me to play in a veterans' game.

Yeah, I'm up for that, I thought, rummaging around for some old kit. *It'll be a laugh.*

But ten minutes into the match, I was struggling. The techniques and tricks I'd been able to execute as a younger bloke were gone and I was horribly off the pace. It wasn't about fitness; I was certainly physically strong enough to compete. Instead, skill-fade had kicked in, an event where certain talents diminish if they're not worked upon for a period of time, ranging from six to eighteen months. In some activities, such as riding a bike, the techniques needed to operate effectively stay burned into our brains because they're so simple. But for other activities – such as tennis, computer programming or mountain climbing – the skills required gradually disappear, but they can be relearned.

Resilience operates in pretty much the same way: it's vital we constantly work on it. We need to find new challenges, escape our comfort zone and seek out areas in which to grow. By reading *Life Under Fire*, either as a whole or in chunks, it will be possible to build an understanding of how to locate, develop and maintain fortitude and emotional grit. Think of the lessons described in here as tools – equipment we can all use in the gym, at home, in the thick of a work mission or while paddling down a bloody great river in the Canadian wilds. But the work, as with any skill, requires practice and commitment.

What's been laid out in this book is adaptable to any situation, and deliberately so. The British military is built to bend and flex in order to overcome all enemies and environments; every individual within it has been taught to prepare for the unexpected, starting with Basic Training before going all the way up to Special Forces Selection. By using Part One, 'The Battle Mind', we can find new ways to overcome any obstacle and grow; with Part Two, 'By Strength and Guile', we're in possession of the artillery required to meet an emotional scrap head-on. Yes, the effort of facing down our demons and challenges will often seem exhausting, but having overcome them we'll eventually emerge stronger. Once it's done, there might even be one or two stories to tell.

As I've explained, life can become a war zone at any given moment. All of us have our deadly ground to cover.

But now you're prepared.

ACKNOWLEDGEMENTS

A lot of hard experience went into the making of *Life Under Fire*. Some of it came from lessons learned in battle; other tactics were picked up during my struggles with mental health as I grew through my recovery. I'd like to thank everybody who has helped to get me to a healthier, happier place today, and to say to everybody dealing with conflicts of their own: victory is always possible, no matter how brutal life gets.

Special mention has to go to the Brotherhood, which features old faces from the UK Special Forces and Royal Marines Commandos, and newer recruits from many different walks of life. Among the roll call of legends are *SAS: Who Dares Wins* teammate and BreakPoint partner Ollie Ollerton, Malcolm Williams and Jamie Sanderson at Rock2Recovery, Aldo Kane, all the lads from *SAS: Who Dares Wins*, and my crew at The Manor. Most of all, I'd like to thank my wife, Jules, and my family – Mum, Dad, Mat and Jamie – for their help in getting me here.

Several people came together to make this book possible. Cheers to all at Transworld – particularly my editor, Henry Vines, my literary agent, Jon Elek, and my *Battle Scars* therapist, Alex Lagaisse, for her bomb-proofing efforts. Finally, I'd like to thank the writer Matt Allen, who somehow captures everything that's rattling around in my brain. Without him this book wouldn't exist, and we've become amazing friends throughout our writing journey.

By strength and guile,

Foxy

London, 2020

Jason Fox joined the Royal Marine Commandos at sixteen, serving for ten years, after which he passed the gruelling selection process for the Special Forces, serving with the Special Boat Service for over a decade and reaching the rank of Sergeant.

Today you are most likely to find him gracing our television screens and giving us a taste of action and adventure around the world.